Praise for *High velocity innovation:*

"If you're developing a physical product, then you must read this book."
—Ian Reilly, chief executive officer, Agersens Pty Ltd

"Required reading for executives and innovation leaders who want to get to market faster and more efficiently while delivering what customers want."
—Benjamin Mimoun Crowe, PhD, head of microphone development, Sonion A/S

"Theory and practice join forces in *High Velocity Innovation* to provide new insights and inspiration to bring innovation to market faster."
—Flemming Moss, senior process consultant, Novo Nordisk Device R&D

High Velocity Innovation

How to Get Your
Best Ideas to Market Faster

KATHERINE RADEKA

Foreword by Roger Johnson

This edition first published in 2019 by Career Press, an imprint of
Red Wheel/Weiser, LLC
With offices at:
65 Parker Street, Suite 7
Newburyport, MA 01950
www.redwheelweiser.com
www.careerpress.com

ISBN: 978-1-63265-156-3
Library of Congress Cataloging-in-Publication Data
available upon request

Cover design by Ellen Varitimos
Interior by Gina Schenck
Typeset in Gill Sans and Minion Pro

Printed in Canada
MAR
10 9 8 7 6 5 4 3 2 1

*To my clients, colleagues, and companions, who know
how to generate pull for a person's best ideas.*

CONTENTS

FOREWORD

If you strive for more relevant innovation or want to outpace your competition, this book is for you.

Whether this is the start of your journey or you are well underway, this book represents the key to unlock the full innovation potential of your teams and organization. The book you are about to read will help you architect and, more importantly, practice the theories you have built about how your teams should work.

As Millard Fuller, cofounder of Habitat for Humanity, said, "It is easier to act yourself into a new way of thinking, than it is to think yourself into a new way of acting." Please remember this as you inventory your current state and prepare to act and deliver the innovation you know your organization needs.

Katherine and I began working together to practice Lean Product Development methods and improve the output of my organization roughly ten years ago. The ideas made total sense, but many associates in my organization had the misconception that "Lean" meant "Less Employees Are Needed," and we struggled to take full advantage of a development system without an embedded culture to support it.

But in the spirit of perfect practice makes perfect, we prioritized and practiced the fundamentals to drive more innovation in shorter cycle times. These techniques are detailed in her first book, *The Mastery of Innovation*. Along the way we realized that we could set aside the word "lean" if it was getting in the way, and we recognized the contribution that Agile could make as long as we were flexible and not purists about it.

More potential existed in the methods than was described or implemented. How might we drive breakthrough levels of innovation output and synchronize at deeper levels in the development organization—Operations, planning, research, and go-to-market strategies—and practice the same methodology to become a learning organization on all accounts, mobilizing quicker and making more effective decisions?

I have had the pleasure of working with Katherine in various capacities at several firms and have been responsible for challenging and changing the way my teams developed products. I have participated in the development and refinement of her methods and have come to rely on them personally to successfully introduce and implement the development philosophy and fundamentals in my organization, leading to aggressive levels of innovation delivery to the market.

Katherine's methods of innovation planning, execution, and maintenance work will help set the framework for High Velocity Innovation. One size does not fit all in product development—especially if you are trying to push the boundaries of what is possible. The Rapid Learning Cycles framework at the center of High Velocity Innovation allows teams to run at their peak efficiency—and then integrate the work to demonstrate the product at all stages of development. It also provides a structure to keep stakeholders informed and participating—without them getting in the way of the real development work.

Katherine also has the voice of experience in implementing the methodologies in practical situations. Be it Sonion, Constellium, or SunPower, the methods are applicable and universally understandable by product developers of all disciplines and backgrounds. This applicability and commonsense acceptance help create a culture of knowledge development and ultimately lead to winning innovation.

Speed in product development wins, but absolute speed is not always the answer. Careful planning, stakeholder buy-in, and risk management at all phases in the program are critical to success. I always believed that my teams had more potential and room to improve, and the methods detailed in this book allow us to improve in the current time, as well as set a framework for continuous improvement in the future.

This book emphasizes successful innovation leadership at all levels and will guide you through the principles and practices, as well as showing which tools can augment the formal (and informal) process for enhanced success.

Remember, innovation has a purpose to accomplish something for your company, your consumers, and your investors. Innovation at the process level will exponentially increase your potential to deliver at the product level. I have witnessed through practice the power of these methods to unite product developers in a common goal to deliver more as a team and organically grow a culture of curious knowledge developers that know how to convert ideas into innovation action.

Developing a product is never an easy endeavor. Today's consumer demands innovation at a never-before-seen pace, at unprecedented quality levels. People inside your firm have ideas as to what these products might be, and even more.

High Velocity Innovation with Rapid Learning Cycles can help break down the challenges and transform your product development machine to be more efficient and effective than you previously thought possible. Rapid Learning Cycles drive time-bound learning to answer the key questions that accelerate innovation by generating pull.

Working in a pull environment is much easier than a push environment for developers (think of pushing a rope) to deliver a consistent pace of breakthrough innovation. Katherine's methods help turn theory into tangible results and actions by generating pull through learning. Dr. Allen Ward of the University of Michigan taught us that learning is the driver of product development. Learning is the engine that drives knowledge and effective decision making. Our teams and organization are knowledge generation factories.

In a physical factory, a scrap pile usually exists for bad parts. While this can be minimized with process control, a nonconforming part can be seen and acted upon. Unfortunately, in our knowledge factory, a bad part (bad knowledge) is harder—if not impossible—to see. This elusive scrap pile can manifest itself later in testing, consumer acceptance, or even worse—a dissatisfied consumer. In the physical factory we strive to eliminate defect-forwarding waste.

Shouldn't we do the same in our knowledge factory? This is precisely why we need time-bound learning cycles for all areas of product development. They give us the chance to learn and evaluate the outcome quickly to eliminate the equivalent of defect-forwarding in our knowledge to make effective decisions.

Innovation cannot be effectively assigned to one special team's deliverables; it needs to permeate the culture of the organization. The goal of a development organization is to be efficient and effective at innovation delivery to make money for shareholders. An effective development organization can create its own oxygen—money to reinvest in more innovation—by showing consistent breakthroughs in its products. This is accomplished through careful cadence planning and execution, both highlighted in this book.

No shortage of development methods exists today. Lean, Agile, Scrum, SAFe®, and Waterfall Stage Gate are great methods, and effective at solving the problem they were designed to solve. As products become more complex, the integration challenge stresses many of these methods, and they begin to break down when pushed to go faster.

No book can be a step-by-step, cookie-cutter, no-thought-required savior manual for success. Every situation is different in our organizations. This book will prompt you to ask yourself critical questions to formulate your plan to deliver High Velocity Innovation. It will help you prioritize goals, learn to build on past learnings and successes, set appropriate metrics, and help you identify the principles, practices, and tools critical to your success.

Most importantly, it will help you establish a culture of innovation. The right mindset and environment for your teams is critical. Strategies can be copied, but execution is a differentiator. Execution is driven by culture.

Promoting a culture that allows controlled failure in safe environments early has helped me personally move faster, but the real breakthrough is to help the organization time-bound investigations to get "scrappy" and learn to use low-resolution or less-than-perfect prototypes to set a direction.

Leaders can create a safety net to allow for experimentation, and a clear Go/No-Go time with options to deliver a constant stream of products. In that environment, you can easily see value-add work versus waste and get to the critical questions quicker at the product level, as well as the planning, process, and people level in your organization.

This book will help you set the framework for the integration of the best methods and help your organization synchronize to go faster. Developers can use the best tool for the job, and your consumer sees a more relevant product faster.

Regardless if you are just starting your journey or if you have been traveling it for a while, this book will help you maximize the potential of your organization through planning, execution, and improvement, but also expecting to go beyond what you thought was possible.

The book you are about to read will help you architect and, more importantly, practice the theory. But it does take practice. Please enjoy this book with that in mind and follow the most important rule for improvement to your innovation output: start today!

Roger Johnson
Senior Vice President
Product Design and Engineering
Keurig Dr Pepper
September 2018

INTRODUCTION

Your company can get its best ideas to market faster.

This may be hard to believe if your products are always late, if your teams don't seem innovative enough, or if new product sales have been disappointing. You may even have experienced a product failure or seen your competitors overtake you.

This may also be hard to believe if your company is an innovation leader, perhaps an iconic innovator like Tesla or Apple. You may have developed processes for innovation that other companies seek to emulate. Yet chances are, there is still a lot of room for improvement.

The companies you'll read about here will show you how they continued to build market leadership by using the practices described in this book to accelerate innovation.

These companies have proven that it is possible to achieve High Velocity Innovation. I know they have been successful because I helped them achieve it and then witnessed their success firsthand. These companies have hundreds of products on the market today that got there faster because of the methods you'll read in this book.

What Is High Velocity Innovation?

High Velocity Innovation is the ability to deliver new solutions that generate value for you and your customers at a rapid pace that is timed to the needs of your customers, markets, and businesses.

An innovation is a novel approach to solving a problem, perhaps one that customers don't know they have. This implies that the innovation is something new—something that's never been done before. It also implies that innovation has a purpose. It's not pure research to advance the state of human knowledge, and it's not pure art for creative expression. It accomplishes something meaningful for your company, your customers, and your investors.

This definition is intentionally broad. It covers new products, services, and business models. It also covers new approaches to manufacturing, supply chains, distribution, human resource management, and finance, because any aspect of a business has opportunities for innovation that delivers business value.

Many of the client examples in this book will describe innovation for new product development, because such innovation programs are the clearest exemplars of the practices that I'll describe. But that's not the only type of innovation that can be accelerated using the practices in this book.

I have seen teams using the High Velocity Innovation system to explore new business models, reinvent supply chains, incorporate Additive Manufacturing production methods, even develop training programs for HR and roll out reorganizations. What they all share is the efforts to develop and deliver a new way to solve a problem for the company and their customers.

Innovation Is Everyone's Responsibility

Innovation is everyone's responsibility, which means that responsibility for innovation cannot be assigned to a specific team or group. Whereas some people are more drawn to projects that extend their industries's frontiers and others prefer to improve the current business, everyone shares responsibility for developing novel ways to solve problems for the company and its customers. Everyone needs the ability to put their best ideas into action without wasting time.

When a company's teams can deliver innovation at a rapid pace, its customers can get access to new, better solutions much faster. Developers spend less time and money fixing problems that arise from outdated information. Investments in research and capital equipment begin generating financial rewards much faster. Marketing and Sales groups can build plans that lead to more successful launches. Competitors find that they cannot keep pace and start falling behind. The best potential new hires are attracted to the company because it is seen as an exciting place to work.

Not every innovation will succeed; the ability to fail fast with bad ideas is just as important as the ability to accelerate successful ideas. Not every innovation needs to be delivered as fast as possible. Companies maximize value from innovation programs by delivering them at the right time: when customers are ready for them. The goal is to increase the company's overall innovation velocity so that the best ideas come to the surface much faster. They receive the support needed for rapid execution so that they get into the market at the right time.

For the past fifteen years, my work has focused on helping companies accelerate innovation, especially the kind of innovation that leads to new products and services. This type of innovation tends to get stuck or take too long. The things teams often do in the name of speeding up such a project only slow innovation down. This book will show you how I helped teams do the right things to achieve innovation at speed.

This book will not address small-scale innovation that leads to continuous improvement or incremental product development. Nor will it focus on ways to generate new ideas; most companies will have more ideas than they can explore once systems and beliefs stop getting in the way. Instead, this book will show you how to get faster at delivering innovations that are bigger, more challenging, and more disruptive wherever they are in your company. There are a lot of myths floating around about how to foster such innovation and the most effective methods are counterintuitive.

Myths About Innovation

One myth is that such innovation necessarily takes a long time. Innovation is knowledge work, and knowledge work expands to fill the available time. If a market researcher is given time and money for a six-month program, she'll scale her research methods to take six months. If you give her three months, she'll scope down the project. If you give her two weeks, she'll pull together whatever she can in such a short time, which may be enough for a preliminary analysis. If you give her an unlimited budget and no deadline, she may never finish. More time does not always equal better results.

Another myth is that innovation teams can't meet deadlines and should not be put on a schedule. The most innovative companies demonstrate time and again that this is not true. Real project plans with real schedules generate pull to get innovation through organizational systems that often put up resistance. The real difference is in the work that's being scheduled and the decisions that arise out of this work. I coach my teams to set hard deadlines for making decisions so that good ideas move fast and bad ideas fail fast.

If all you take away from this book is the need to expect innovation teams to move quickly and to hold them accountable for meeting dates, then you can accelerate innovation for the teams that you lead. But you don't have to figure this out by yourself. You can leverage the experiences of the companies in this book to give your teams the support structures needed to move fast.

Fast Innovation Is Effective Innovation

When an innovation team moves fast, they stay light on their feet and adapt more readily to change. When they are held accountable for meeting goals with real dates, they have the urgency they need to stay focused when everything else seems to be more important. They are less likely to get stuck on unworkable ideas and more likely to embrace creative ideas that lead to breakthroughs.

The information they gather in the early phases of a program will still be relevant in the later phases. The early-look customers they use to help them define the product are still excited about it at launch time. It's much easier for executive sponsors to stay actively engaged because they see lots of visible progress. The entire innovation system is tuned for speed from idea to launch.

The System for High Velocity Innovation

A company is ready for High Velocity Innovation when it has:

- **A strategic imperative and objectives for innovation that are cascaded down to the entire organization.** When your entire company is centered around the need for innovation and the results your company can achieve with innovation, it's easier for managers to protect the investments you make in innovation from competing needs and it's easier for the innovators to make better decisions.

- **Innovation teams and Team Leaders that can draw upon the company's shared knowledge base.** High Velocity Innovation can't take place in a vacuum because teams don't have time for reinvention. The best teams draw from the existing businesses so that they can leverage as much as possible, even if the final product looks completely different.

- **An Innovation Process that provides high accountability and high responsiveness.** Since knowledge work expands to fill the available time, teams need firm deadlines, expectations, and sponsor engagement to help them make good decisions that stick. Your teams move faster and deliver better results when you have high expectations and eliminate anything that gets in the way.

- **Explicit strategies for leveraging innovations into new platforms and product families that can be replicated in other parts of the business and extended into new businesses.** This ensures that a company derives maximum value from new ideas and provides a launch platform for a stream of innovations. Your investment in platforms builds competitive advantage that is hard for others to reverse engineer.

- **Actionable metrics that build accountability and visibility.** Good KPIs for innovation acknowledge the risks and rewards inherent in things that are new and different while providing accountability for the work necessary to evaluate and then execute an idea. When you can show your company's leaders and your peers that your teams are getting better results, they gain more confidence in your teams' ability to deliver.

With these elements in place, your team will be poised to find new ideas, identify the best of those to carry into development, and move from investigation to execution rapidly.

Build an Innovation System for High Velocity

This book will share how to put these elements in place to achieve High Velocity Innovation. It will give you ideas to build into a hypothesis for how innovation should work at your company, and then it will help you design experiments to test your theory.

These small-scale experiments will demonstrate that High Velocity Innovation is achievable at your company, and give you guidelines for how to move from experimentation into full-scale execution. When you're ready, you'll know what you need to achieve High Velocity Innovation everywhere that you need it.

You can get your best ideas to market faster with High Velocity Innovation.

PART ONE

WHY YOUR COMPANY NEEDS
HIGH VELOCITY INNOVATION

CHAPTER ONE

Why Innovation Programs Take Too Long

On September 2, 2015, Elon Musk announced on Twitter that Tesla was moving out of the margins and into the mainstream of the car industry. The Tesla 3 would be the company's first car for the masses, with a price comparable to a low-end luxury car. It would incorporate all the innovation that Tesla was known for and it was expected to revolutionize the car industry.

When the first one rolled off the line in July of 2017, Tesla had a backlog of 455,000 orders to fulfill. However, the company missed its first production target. And then missed the second. As months passed, one problem after another plagued production.

Savvy consumers know that production problems at launch often mean quality problems later. In March of 2018, Tesla recalled half the cars it produced for a steering wheel repair. The backlog of Tesla 3 orders gave Tesla some buffer to address the problems, but the markets were not so forgiving. Tesla's stock dropped from a peak of $383 per share in June of 2017 to a low of $252 in April of 2018.

The company's iconic reputation for innovation and Elon Musk's credibility as one of the most innovative persons in the world came under serious threat. No one doubted that the Tesla 3 was innovative, but now the execution failures would blunt the impact this innovation would have on the car industry.

How did this happen to one of the most innovative companies in the world? As Elon Musk said in an interview for *Bloomberg News* in July of 2018, "We were huge idiots and didn't know what we were doing."[1]

Innovation Management Is Counterintuitive

Effective innovation development is the ability to drive an innovation to completion, whether it's a new product, process, or business model. Yet innovation management is counterintuitive because common assumptions about management tend to break down in environments of high uncertainty. This means the things that teams do to speed up innovation often slow it down.

At Tesla, Musk had designed the Tesla 3 and its production process on the assumption that the factory would be as fully automated as possible, and then jumped with both feet into building a fully automated factory. Yet that meant incorporating a lot of unproven ideas about how to automate manufacturing all at once before the product had been stabilized and proven.

Tesla invested hundreds of millions of dollars in robots that sat idle after it became clear that people could do the same thing with less cost, time, and quality problems. They made a lot of costly decisions without the knowledge to make those decisions, and paid dearly for it in reputation, market capitalization, and consumer confidence. Although Tesla's struggles were the ones that made the newspapers, many Innovation Program Leaders deal with these same issues behind the scenes while trying to do their best to go as fast as they can.

Innovation Program Leaders Try to Do the Right Thing

It seems like the best thing to do with a new business idea is to run it by some customers to get reactions and then make decisions based on their feedback. But customers are notoriously bad at providing accurate feedback on something that's in the conceptual stage. Most customers can't give good information about a new idea until it is made more concrete with a representative sample of the final product. And in some industries, like food and beverage or medical devices, it may not be possible to give customers representative samples for something that has never been done before, for safety reasons.

In product development, it seems right to define all the requirements up front and then drive them into execution with a streamlined development process. However, that assumes teams have good information, and that's not possible to get so early in the program. If the execution team assumes that requirements are frozen and acts accordingly, then changes to requirements become expensive rework loops. For innovation programs, the requirements change often as new information comes in.

Innovators deal with a lot of uncertainty, and it seems like making bold decisions early is one way to reduce the amount of turbulence. But those bold decisions are the ones that lead to major failures like the production process for the Tesla 3, that trigger massive delays and cost overruns, if the product survives at all. Instead of accelerating innovation, they slow it down.

The Things People Do to Speed Up Innovation Slow It Down

Over and over again, I see the things company leaders do to accelerate innovation often slow it down instead. They encourage teams to be decisive, only to find that many of those decisions have to be revisited later, when it's expensive to change the decisions. They accelerate the Investigation Phases of innovation to meet an aggressive time line, and then find that the Execution Phases get bogged down. They staff an innovation team with outsiders for fresh thinking and then wonder why these teams' products cost too much or fail to resonate with consumers. Figure 1.1 shows the problems that people experience over and over when they try to push innovation.

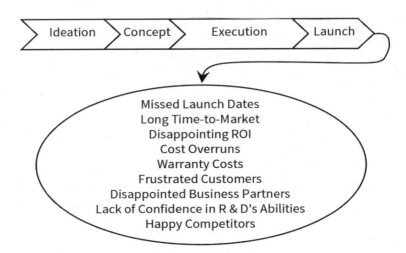

Figure 1.1: Disappointing results from innovation.

Three practices in particular receive a lot of praise in innovation management literature. They have been around long enough that if they had a lot of success, they'd be much more common with many innovations in the market that would demonstrate their value. Although a lot of theory has been written about them as compelling hypotheses, they don't have much evidence to prove them.

Skunkworks

Conventional wisdom says that if a company's people are not innovative and the processes and metrics conspire to kill innovation, the best thing to do is to get it completely out of the building. "Skunkworks" refers to a team that has been deliberately isolated from the company's core and told to "do all the new things we can't do" or "start with a blank sheet of paper." Figure 1.2 shows how isolated they are from their peers in the business.

They're usually located in a remote building or an independent space rather than sitting with their Engineering and Marketing peers. Some innovation authors write as if this idea is a new discovery, but that's where storied innovation engines like PARC, HP Labs, and Bell Labs came from.

There's a reason why these entities have become shadows of their former selves: they were not very effective at delivering innovations that their sponsoring companies could implement, and therefore they became targets for funding cuts. PARC's best inventions, the mouse and the touchscreen, were exploited by Apple, not Xerox. Bell Labs spun out a few successful companies when the parent company was willing to support them, but the breakup of AT&T also broke up their funding for such wide-ranging research. HP Labs incubated a lot of ideas throughout the decades while the founders were still alive and able to keep the teams focused. After they retired, funding evaporated as a series of downsizings and management missteps led to the need to shore up shareholder results.

Figure 1.2: Skunkworks teams are isolated from the current business.

Even the more recent examples are just as likely to show spin-offs or killed ideas rather than new initiatives that truly create value for the companies that sponsored them.

It turns out that companies, especially the large, well-funded companies that can afford skunkworks teams, have powerful immune systems. Since the people in such efforts are cut off from the rest of the organization in every way but funding and a tenuous connection to leadership, there is no home for the innovations when they come back into the company.

Either these teams develop into standalone entities that are ripe for being cancelled, sold off, or spun off, or they might as well. They have nothing in common with the parent company. At some point, the investment stops making sense. All their management sponsors have to do is change the strategy or leave the company, and all that investment gets put to waste.

Specialist Innovation Teams

Even worse are the proponents of assigning responsibility for innovation to a specialist team, mainly consisting of people brought in from outside the company. At least most companies staff skunkworks teams with experienced people. The Innovation Specialist approach is fun for the people on the innovation teams because they are freed from much accountability or need to learn about their new company, and encouraged to do things that are dramatically different than the corporate norms. But it doesn't ensure that the teams will get better results and the track record backs that up.

Figure 1.3: Dedicated innovation teams push irrelevant ideas.

This approach seems to be especially popular with those who study innovation practices academically, who base their hypotheses on the observed externalities of innovation programs. Like skunkworks, these programs don't have a good empirical record of success. In fact, such teams can become deaf to valid constructive criticism from the company's experienced personnel, who may have good points even though they appear to be resistant to change. Figure 1.3 shows that the information flow from such teams to the current business tends to be a one-way push.

On the other side, it sends the wrong message to everyone else: "You're part of the past but not the future, and as such, you have no responsibility to be innovative." Some people will love the freedom to pursue an undemanding status quo and others will chafe at the restrictions; either way, the company is not getting the best from its most deeply knowledgeable people.

Startup Innovation for Corporate R&D

Finally, many innovation team leads like the idea of "going back to the garage" and embracing the methods that allow startups to become multi-billion-dollar businesses. But a corporate innovation team, even in a small established company, has both strengths and weaknesses that a startup doesn't have.

In Chapter 3, you'll read about some aspects of Lean Startup that translate well into corporate innovation programs, but these tools are not dependent upon building a startup culture. Today, people who want to work in startups have ample opportunities to work for one or even start one. Even there, the heavy workload is not sustainable and burns people out.

The people who work in a corporate environment have chosen to work in a place with more constraints and stability but fewer sacrifices, but that doesn't mean they lack good ideas. Such an approach almost ensures that people with families, especially but not exclusively women, will be locked out of innovation programs and the career advancement they can foster because the demands will be even heavier.

All of that might be worth it if it delivered better results. Here, the evidence again shows scant progress toward improving the velocity of innovation. Figure 1.4 shows that such a model combines the worst aspects of the skunkworks model and the dedicated innovation team model: the group is "protected" from the current business and exempted from much of the rules, yet they are expected to push ideas onto the rest of the company.

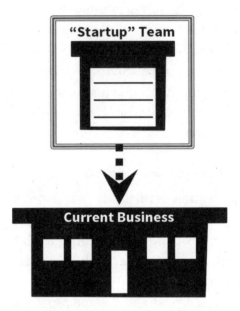

Figure 1.4: "Start-up" teams are isolated and push irrelevant ideas.

I witnessed this firsthand when I was part of the short-lived E-Services Inside Factory at HP Labs. This was an attempt to go "back to the garage" to reinvent how services talked to each other over the Internet, an early form of the API frameworks that drive tools like Zapier. At the time, e-services were a core part of HP's strategy, and the assignment seemed like it would be a lot of fun.

Yet strong executive support led to lack of accountability and the freedom to do anything, which made it hard to get anything meaningful done, and there was no place to commercialize the interesting stuff we did manage to build. I was relieved when I moved back to the core printer business, which needed innovation and knew how to deliver it.

Tesla demonstrates these perils, because delivering a new mass market car is very different from delivering a new service, or even a limited-edition sports car. Tesla's development process, still grounded in the founder-centric worldview of the startup, inadequately met the challenges that this mainstream car presented about how to scale up production volumes and lower cost.

Wrong Methods for Innovation

All of these methods share three faulty assumptions about innovation, and none of them address the real reasons why innovation programs take too long and deliver disappointing results. These assumptions are compelling because they are all partially true. But remedies that address them only attack the symptoms of slow innovation—not the root causes—and ultimately do more harm than good.

Faulty Assumption #1

The normal corporate culture and many employees get in the way of innovation.

This is the driving assumption that says innovation teams need protection, and it's salient because it's partly true. Most corporate environments don't support innovation, and most people in any given company don't have the burning desire to be innovative. But the solution isn't found when companies build walls around small teams of outsiders, which takes away accountability for meeting corporate norms, and then expect magic to happen.

But it is easier than admitting that the real cause is lack of leadership pull for innovation. When the need for innovation becomes obvious because the company is falling behind, it's easier for leaders to seek solutions outside the company than rekindle the spirit of innovation inside the company. But that accelerates the decline of the core business with no guarantees that outside innovation can be successfully integrated back inside.

The truth behind the myth is that your teams won't think of themselves as innovators if they don't believe they can innovate or don't think it's part of the jobs. If you complain, "We're not innovative" or "We're not creative" within hearing distance of your teams, you just created a self-fulfilling prophesy.

A subset of your employee base is less comfortable with change and uncertainty. You don't want these people to be assigned to work on innovation all the time. But it is reasonable to expect that they contribute to innovation within their areas of expertise, and that when they do, they will be recognized and rewarded.

Companies that achieve High Velocity Innovation seek to rekindle the spark of entrepreneurship inside everyone, at least to some degree. They generate pull for innovation with a corporate strategy and cascading objectives that place responsibility for innovation within every team. Then they build a culture of high accountability to ensure that innovation remains a top priority even when leaders' instincts tell them the current business takes precedence.

Faulty Assumption #2

Leaders have to build walls around innovators to protect them (from their leaders).

Another reason why these ineffective methods are so intuitive is because leaders following corporate norms will kill innovations to protect the current business, through neglect if not through sabotage. This is a real concern and a pattern that I've seen over and over again.

When a production line goes down for the company's cash cow, everyone jumps in to fix it. When a major customer has a need, the company will do its utmost to fulfill that need, or else a competitor will. This means that innovation programs are repeatedly starved for resources as people and money get redeployed to shore up the current business.

Innovation programs need to be protected from this, but not with walls. Instead, high accountability for delivering innovation needs to be built into the organizational design with strategy, team structures, metrics, performance goals, and budgets that provide resources for innovation.

These elements generate a greater ability to stay the course on innovations even when the current business is screaming for resources. Unless the company's survival is at stake, the innovation programs continue. Even then, innovative thinking can make the difference between prosperity and bankruptcy.

Innovations, or at least the ones worth more than just a "go do it" decision, operate on a longer time line than incremental product development or continuous improvement. It takes time for an innovation to prove itself and the corporate incentives system must account for that.

Companies achieve high velocity by aligning leadership on the need for innovation, and ensuring that intrinsic and extrinsic incentives line up with the need to deliver innovations. Executives need to be held accountable for delivering innovation in a way that's appropriate for their responsibilities, and anything that rewards sabotage or neglect must be removed.

Faulty Assumption #3

Teams need to run innovation programs differently.

It is true that innovation programs, especially those that require new business models or scientific breakthroughs, can take a long time to mature, and some of this timing is unpredictable. It's much easier to predict how long it will take to do something and what the results will be if only one or two elements are new to the company. The management methods used for innovation programs need to accommodate such uncertainty.

That doesn't mean an innovation team should be allowed to make its own rules or refuse to play by any rules. There is no advantage for the innovation team, and it tells everyone else to turn off their innovation engines. Instead, teams need adaptations of the existing rules that preserve the company's language and frameworks while providing flexibility where innovation teams need it. That way, innovation programs will be easier to move through execution, which will require cross-functional collaboration.

Innovation teams are good places to conduct experiments with new ways of working, and the results of their experiments will be illuminating for the whole company. If they experiment with sit/stand desks and get better results, chances are that other teams will benefit when they make these changes. This sends the message that innovation teams are sources for good ideas that the entire company can leverage.

The Root Causes of Slow Innovation

If the three assumptions I just reviewed are faulty or incomplete and fixing them doesn't accelerate innovation, what does? You need to go deeper to find the leverage points at which making changes will lead to faster innovation. Here are the areas that your company's innovation system must address if you want to achieve High Velocity Innovation.

Root Cause #1

Decision making in the fog of uncertainty is inherently difficult.

The decisions made early in an Innovation Program have lasting consequences. Decisions about business partners and target markets can come back to hurt teams later as more information becomes known. Teams won't have the information they need to make good decisions without a lot of research, and even then, they don't know if an underlying assumption will prove to be true. Yet when such a decision must be revisited later, it can have dramatic impacts on schedule and cost of the final product. Sometimes the revisited decisions invalidate the entire business case.

To accelerate innovation, your teams must do something that few corporate systems reinforce: delay major decisions as long as they can. They need to pursue multiple options for their major decisions, gather as much information as they can early in the process, and then keep those options open for as long as possible.

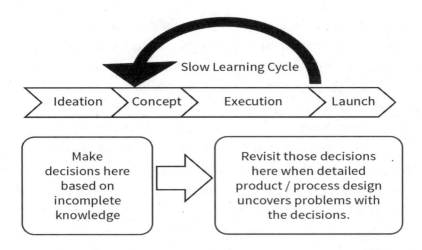

Figure 1.5: Revisited decisions lead to long, slow learning cycles.

This process allows time for your teams to gather more complete information, allows time for their assumptions to be validated, and allows time for any "unknown unknowns" to emerge. This won't prevent 100 percent of an innovation team's major decisions from the need to be revisited in the Execution Phases, but eliminating some of them can accelerate innovation by reducing the overall burden on the execution team.

In Part 2, this book will introduce program management methods and KPIs that cut through the fog to help teams and their sponsors make better decisions at the right time.

Root Cause #2

Accountability and measurement increase the fog.

The ways most companies measure innovation doesn't improve decision making. They either measure innovation programs the way they measure traditional programs, with ROI calculations that reward short-term payback and process metrics that reward conformance to schedule at a task level. Or they fail to measure them at all because "there are no rules/ the rules don't apply."

Your executives need windows of visibility into the progress of an Innovation Program that are different than the ones needed for a traditional product development program. You need to be able to see that the group is hitting critical benchmarks in technical development or adoption rates.

In an environment of high uncertainty, conformance to schedule and budget at a detailed level tells you almost nothing. These numbers will be much worse than they would be for a typical program, so the executive's intuitive grasp of the numbers will be far off from reality. These numbers will increase the fog of uncertainty rather than decrease it, and increase executive angst about innovation rather than give your teams confidence.

Innovation teams need metrics, including Key Performance Indicators around schedules and budgets, that are appropriate for the phase of the work. Chapter 9 will outline the metrics that help innovation teams and their leaders understand where they are and where they need to go next.

Root Cause #3

Innovation is always less urgent than the current business.

Innovation, especially forward-looking innovation, is always less urgent than the current business. When a manufacturing line is down, it's going to be all hands on deck until the line gets back up. And when company results are not meeting expectations, it's often the innovation teams that take the hit.

There's no point in blaming anyone for this; it has to do with the way our brains are wired. Human beings are great at putting out fires; somewhat good at preventing them by eliminating the obvious sources they see in the moment (like a candle too close to a curtain); and not good at dealing with long-term threats that increase the likelihood of fire (like letting an old electrical system get overloaded).

Chapter 4 will describe how strategy and cascading objectives build urgency for innovation so that it maintains priority in the face of current business needs.

The Core Problem: Lack of Pull for Innovation

The core problem with innovation in established companies is that there is a lack of pull for it at every level. At the executive level, leaders go away on strategic retreats to define grand strategies but then manage as if short-term results are all that matter. Middle managers try to protect their groups from the demands and failures of innovation programs by keeping their heads down and focusing only on the current business. Individual contributors find that their best ideas get ignored and innovation projects are on the bottom of the priority list. Skunkworks team members find themselves isolated from their peers who are working on the current business, and lack the critical voices they need to avoid making big mistakes.

This may seem like a culture problem, but efforts to change a company culture rarely achieve the results that leaders hope for. As Roger said in the foreword, "It's easier to act your way to a new way of thinking than think your way to a new way of acting."

The companies included in this book found that they get better results from efforts to increase innovation with a coherent strategy, protected funding but fluid resources, and trained Innovation Managers with teams of flexible resources and tools, which can do a lot to increase the pace of innovation and rebuild a company's confidence.

If your child believed he was getting bad grades because he was a poor student, you wouldn't think you could solve the problem just by changing your child's beliefs about school. You'd get him a tutor, help out more with his homework, and help him build better study habits. You'd look to see if perhaps there wasn't something else like bullying or a learning disability that was getting in the way. You'd know that your child will believe he's a better student when he's getting better grades, and probably not before.

People Become Innovative by Delivering Innovation

Just like your child's grades, the same thing is true for innovation. If you want your people to believe they are innovative and to deliver more innovation, you have to create the conditions for innovation and provide them with the support they need to be more successful. This is the approach that worked for the companies I've helped, and we have many successful innovation launches to demonstrate that this works.

Tesla's production challenges bruised the company's reputation for delivering innovation, and Musk has lost some of his luster as an innovation icon. But to his credit, Musk has accepted personal responsibility for the failures that sent the company to "production hell" and continues to reiterate his belief in the company's overarching vision. His comments sustain the pull for innovation that can help his teams get through this rough time, and emerge believing in themselves as innovators who can deliver. By the fourth quarter of 2018, Tesla had cut the time it took to build the Model 3 by more than 30 percent, and missed quarterly production projections by only 2,000 units out of 86,500.[2]

The way to build a culture of innovation is to deliver your company's best ideas to market faster, and the way to do that is to ensure you've generated pull for innovation.

Your Next Actions

- ☐ List examples of recent innovation programs at your company, whether or not they succeeded. Reflect on the areas in which these programs struggle.

- ☐ Ask a few of your colleagues, especially those from Marketing or Sales, how innovative your company is perceived to be. Are you a market leader, a fast follower, or falling behind?

- ☐ Look at who has responsibility for generating ideas and evaluating concepts. Ask a few members of that team how easily they can transfer the good concepts to their partners, and what obstacles they encounter.

CHAPTER TWO

Keurig Dr Pepper's At Home appliance group has two major market windows to sell into: the spring season ahead of Mother's Day and the fall season to set up for holiday sales. The need to get products to Keurig's resellers in time for these events creates strong pull to drive product development to completion on time. Missing a key date with a major reseller can mean missing an entire season of sales. Such a group thrives when they can align their Innovation Processes around these pull signals, to deliver the right product to the market at the right time. When such an Innovation Process is functioning well, the company can control the timing of new innovation releases. Teams can maximize impact in the market by leveraging the power of pull.

Innovation Velocity Starts with a Strong Pull

"Pull" is how your company's desires (as manifested in its strategies), organizational structures, processes, systems, tools, and metrics brings forth the innovation it needs. That need can come from a market opportunity, a competitive threat, a compelling vision for the company's future direction, or even the risk that the entire business could be disrupted and made obsolete. Whatever it is, the pull must be to be strong enough to bring your entire company into alignment around the need for innovation.

Examples of pull are all around us. If you've ever eaten a bowl of spaghetti or long rice noodles, you've probably seen what happens when you pull the noodles from the bowl. Whether you grasp a few with chopsticks or with a fork, the moment you begin pulling them out of the bowl, you see that the strands of noodles untangle themselves and move into alignment with each other. Then you can wrap them around the fork or put them in a spoon to make them easier to eat.

Trying to push noodles onto a fork doesn't work all that well; they stay tangled up, keep falling off, and it's hard to get just the amount that you want. By pulling them out of the bowl, you can get the right amount to put into your mouth, and do it without making a mess.

You can see the same force at work when you use magnets to bring iron filings into alignment, or when you watch a field of poppies rotate together so that they're always facing the sun. An attractive force is pulling a number of disorganized, separate things into alignment with each other and the pulling force.

Once an innovation team has alignment, all the energy put into the team moves in one direction and team members can go much faster with less effort.

It's Not Easy to Push Spaghetti—or Innovation

When an innovation team gets too separated from the core organization and then tries to push ideas on the rest of the company, they face a lot of resistance. It's tempting to blame the people inside the larger company for being "too focused on the current business" or "too set in their ways." But no one likes having things pushed to them, especially those things that they don't understand and didn't want in the first place. Figure 2.1 shows how tangled up things can get when teams try to push innovation on other teams.

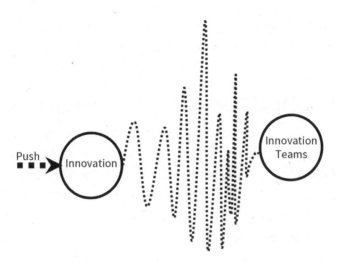

Figure 2.1: The problem with push.

This is why open-ended innovation programs take so long to get to market, why innovation teams are so vulnerable to being reassigned at the first sign of trouble, and why people claim that it's difficult for a mature company to be innovative. There is a lot of "push" from innovation champions and little "pull" from the rest of the company. The energy put into innovation goes in a lot of directions at once, and the team has difficulty achieving high velocity.

It's better to create the conditions for the company to pull innovation across organizational boundaries so that the innovation team spends less energy pushing and the execution team spends less energy resisting. That requires a compelling need for innovation, along with an innovation system that reinforces the need. All the energy goes in one direction, and the team can move a lot faster. The reinforcement begins in the idea stage and sustains itself until the idea is in execution. Figure 2.2 shows the different ways that a company can generate pull for innovation.

In a fast-moving consumer products company like Keurig, the need to meet reseller dates helps to pull the work of product development through. Industries that often struggle with time-to-market lack that strong external pull from the market. If your company is in a market without natural customer pull, one of the first things you can do to improve time-to-market is to create external pull from a trade show, a codevelopment program with a major customer, or a commitment to investors.

Pull Makes It Easier to Get Hard Things Done

The Camino de Santiago is a set of medieval pilgrimage routes in Spain that long-distance walkers follow to this day. All of the routes converge upon Santiago de Compostela; tradition says that the bones of St. James the Great, one of the Twelve Apostles, are buried there. People who have walked the Camino say that once they start, they feel a strong force pulling them toward Santiago.

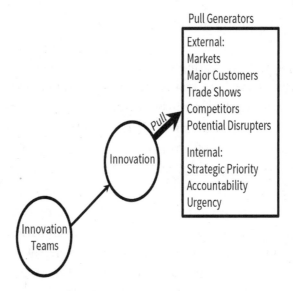

Figure 2.2: The power of pull.

Maybe it's all the others who are walking in the same direction, maybe it's the fact that all the arrows they see point them in that direction, or maybe it is the shared encouragement to accomplish something so difficult. Whatever it is, people claim that this feeling makes them get up early and start down the trail in the morning and continue walking through blisters, soreness, and fatigue. That's the kind of pull companies need for their programs to increase innovation velocity.

Innovation teams have to overcome a lot in order to execute on innovation: resistance to change, competition for resources, the perception that the new idea is a threat, short-term results orientation, and the need to keep current customers happy. They will encounter obstacles they didn't expect, unrealistic expectations and miscommunication with key stakeholders, periods when visible progress is hard to see, and times when experiments don't generate the results they had hoped.

External pull is important but not sufficient. Many consumer market-driven companies rush to get new products to market that have had features stripped out that could not be finished in time, nagging quality issues that couldn't be fixed in the initial production run, or last-minute changes that drove up cost of goods sold (COGS) and cut into profits.

The team may have a track record of getting products out on time, but the products disappoint customers, investors, and the developers. To accelerate innovation, company leaders need to generate internal pull that starts from the beginning of an Innovation Program.

Internal Pull Accelerates Innovation

The way to prevent these issues is to generate internal pull for innovation earlier in the program, so that the team has time to learn what they need to know before they go into execution, which is when they commit to a specific release date or market window. This is true regardless of whether the Innovation Process will lead to a new business, a new product, or a new Supply Chain Management System. The "fuzzy front end" is the part of the development process that needs the most attention if you are going to accelerate innovation because that's when the team makes decisions that drive success during the Execution Phase.

Keurig's product development teams generate pull for innovation early in the process by defining what's New, Unique, or Difficult (NUD) about a given product, and how teams will leverage existing technology platforms. This helps the team focus on the aspects of a product that they need to investigate early to prevent problems later.

Keurig's leaders on the commercial side and the Engineering side require teams to identify these NUDs before moving into the Learning

Phase of a program, and then require teams to demonstrate that they solved these NUDS before moving into execution. The Innovation Process pulls the innovation required to solve these NUDs out of the team, and resolving these NUDs ahead of execution reduces the risk that they will become problems in late development, which will cost time and resources.

A Good Innovation Process Pulls Innovation Early

The following are requirements of an innovation system that is capable of building internal pull for innovation when it will accelerate innovation the most.

Strategic Priority

Innovation programs are often the first things cut when a company looks to improve its cost structures or runs into trouble. On the surface, it makes sense to protect the current business. That is where the cash comes from to satisfy current investors and make investments in new ventures. When a manufacturing line goes down, a company has to issue a recall or the company needs to cut costs in response to slow sales, and the innovation team is the place to look for resources that can be redeployed.

Yet when a company focuses only on the current business without sustaining its investments in innovation, everyone from leadership down to the shop floor loses confidence in the company's ability to innovate. When a company's most innovative people say, "We can't be innovative," it stems from the experiences they had when they tried to do something new. If they can't get funding or their teams are too fragmented to make any progress, then it becomes easier for them to stop innovating or to leave for a company at which their ideas can be realized.

In extreme cases, companies sign their own death warrants by taking actions like these. When the company is struggling because the current business model is not viable in the long term, then starving innovation programs only accelerates the company's decline, tying it even more closely to a way of doing business that is not sustainable and creating space for outside innovators to find opportunities for disruption that they can exploit.

When your company has increased innovation velocity by building strong pull for innovation, it's much easier for innovation teams to maintain their dedicated resources, and receive the assistance they need from other functions. They're seen as a group that delivers results quickly, instead of a long-term investment.

Everyone within your company recognizes that delivering on innovation is a strategic priority that is intended to build the company's future. It becomes easier for everyone in the company to protect the time, money, and resources that are dedicated to innovation because they understand that the company's visions, goals, and plans cannot be met any other way, and that the teams are moving as fast as they can to deliver results.

Keurig has made its strategy for its appliance business so clear to its developers that all the teams I encountered there had no problem tying their product back to the strategy. They could all tell me how their products would help the company achieve its strategic goals in concrete terms.

I helped them refine this into a Core Hypothesis for the product that crystallized their product's strategic intent down to a testable hypothesis about how this product would build value for Keurig and for its customers and consumers. That helps a team understand what it needs to demonstrate during the Learning Phase to validate the hypothesis, which leads them to get more clear about their NUDs. I'll share more about the Core Hypothesis in Chapter 4.

Accountability for Results

Priority comes with accountability for delivering results from innovation. Whether your company strives to innovate by creating a new business, delivering innovative products, or by innovating around its internal processes to reduce costs and increase efficiencies, people need to be held accountable for delivering results and achieving strategic objectives.

The people who are entrusted with the Innovation Process need to be measured and rewarded differently than the people who are responsible for running the current business. However, no one should be exempt from the need to innovate (that is, seek better ways to do things) even in areas like production or customer service that don't seem to be ripe areas for new ideas. In fact, sometimes a company's most important innovations have more to do with new ways to handle distribution (Amazon) or supply chains (Nike).

Not all ideas will succeed, and not all ideas should succeed. Innovation Programs have to sift through a lot of so-so ideas to find the best ones. You can't hold people accountable for the success or failure of any single idea in the early phases. In fact, a fast failure is something to celebrate.

Accountability in this context is the responsibility to identify the best ideas using effective methods and drive those through execution. By defining ownership in this way, we allow for times when the innovation team comes up dry.

Responsibility that Extends Through Execution

At the same time, innovation teams can't just go on vacation when they transfer an idea to an execution team for the "boring" work of implementation. An innovative idea gets proven in the Execution Phases, and the team responsible for identifying the best ideas is also accountable for how effectively they selected the best ideas, transferred those ideas into execution teams, and drove execution to completion. The time to reach successful launch is the true measure of innovation velocity.

When an innovation team and its partners understand the need to increase innovation velocity and have the structures to support faster innovation, accountability for executing innovation becomes more concrete. They are measured on the ability to deliver visible progress on an aggressive time line, not a fuzzy future that's still far away from being achieved.

This is especially helpful for those groups outside the innovation team that need to support innovation alongside the current business. It becomes part of what they are expected to do, not something "extra" that they can do if they have time. The innovation team experiences better alignment between the team's expectations for delivering results and how the team is measured and rewarded. They have a stronger sense of urgency to achieve the results they need to deliver.

At Keurig, they started to tie performance bonuses to a development team's success at hitting the cost, delivery date, and key feature set commitments at the start of the Execution Phase. This has encouraged teams to delay the start of this phase until they had the knowledge to make these commitments with confidence. The net impact has been to pull learning forward where it takes less time and resources, so that the team can move fast in the Execution Phase without encountering as many roadblocks that would kill their momentum.

Urgency

Innovation has an inherently longer time scale than most corporate activities. The natural human tendency, reinforced by corporate norms, is to focus on an activity with a short-term deadline or payoff. Even if innovation team members don't get sidetracked with short-term emergencies, there is still not much urgency to get innovation work done.

Innovation teams work best when they explore lots of ideas with short, focused experiments that have clear time boundaries. The structure increases the chances that some of their ideas will survive. If the investigation leads to a program that will take a long time to execute, such as building an entirely new line of business, the team still needs to have clear expectations and time boundaries with frequent reviews.

Knowledge work expands to fill the available time. To counter this, build urgency into the expectations for innovation teams by expecting them to work at high velocity. When a company pulls innovation through to execution, then the people who work on these innovations have a sense of urgency that helps set appropriate time boundaries. These time boundaries help the teams show more visible progress, and that helps teams build up momentum to carry a project over a rough spot, or through a time of extreme uncertainty.

In Chapter 6, I'll introduce the concept of Rapid Learning Cycles to build this urgency into the development process by placing innovation within clear time boundaries. At Keurig, all innovation teams use Rapid Learning Cycles for the earliest phases of the program. The first products that used this process show how they hit the Execution Phase in a much better position than previous programs, with less risk and fewer outstanding unknowns left to solve.

Rapid, Honest Feedback

Innovation velocity isn't just felt within the team; it's also felt by the leadership team that gives the innovation team a greater share of its time and attention. That makes it easier for the leadership team to go on the innovation team's journey with them, so that the team gets rapid feedback from leadership about the direction they're headed. Yet some executives think that the best approach is to leave an innovation team alone.

Some innovation programs waste away because the team has been given money, resources, and time to push an idea onto the rest of the company. However, no one likes to have things pushed at them, and therefore resist the attempts to get them interested. This is especially true if nothing else in the company is generating a need for High Velocity Innovation.

This forces the innovation team to become salespeople, always extolling the good aspects of their idea and minimizing the bad aspects. They sell to senior leaders to maintain their budget and resources, they sell to internal and external partners to get the help they need, and they sell to themselves to justify the investments of time and hard work that they're putting into it.

But this only makes the problems and obstacles more difficult to find, even if the team is not actively covering them up. The team cannot risk getting honest feedback because then they failed to sell their idea. It's easier to work in isolation to solve problems without help so that their final presentation looks as good as possible, in the hopes that they can get someone to care about it.

A company with high innovation velocity is one that can also look at individual innovation efforts more honestly and one that is motivated to look at them more frequently. Since innovation has value and downstream teams are eager for new ideas, the Innovation Program's success does not hinge on the success of any one innovation. An innovator's job is not at risk for telling the truth.

The Rapid Learning Cycles framework provides a mechanism for getting feedback from sponsors and other leaders via Integration Events, during which major program decisions are made and the leadership team has an opportunity to steer the team. At Keurig, a team will never go more than twelve weeks without an opportunity to get rapid honest feedback, and most teams get feedback at least every six weeks during the most crucial learning phases when NUDs are being solved. That generates a lot of pull to accelerate innovation through uncertainty.

A Clear Path to Follow Through Uncertainty

Innovation is an inherently high-risk activity with a lot of uncertainty. If a team already knew how to do the things that they're exploring, they would have already done them or decided not to do them. Some teams compare the uncertainty of these early phases to running rapids on a river swollen with snow melt. The water is choppy, the rocks underneath look deadly, and the currents are swirling in unpredictable ways around the obstacles in the river.

Rafters know that the way through such rapids is to keep paddling. By building up velocity ahead of the rapids and maintaining it in the rapids, they keep the raft pointed downriver and build up momentum they can use to control the raft as they maneuver it around obstacles. The momentum pulls the raft through the rapids.

When a company expects and supports increased innovation velocity, they give a team both momentum and a clear path to follow so that they don't get tangled up in all the obstacles they have to overcome. It's easier to anticipate the problems and it's easier to steer around them. When they are able to generate both internal and external pull, they have the means to develop an innovation system that delivers its best ideas to the market faster. Figure 2.3 shows what such a system looks like.

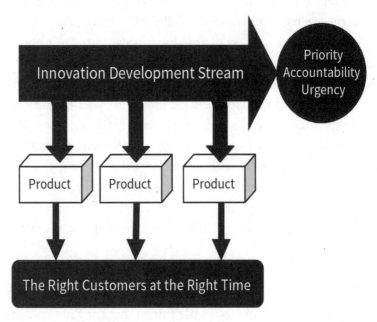

Figure 2.3: The pull-based innovation system.

This is something that innovation experts have known for a long time, and the next chapter will discuss how others have attempted to generate pull with practices from Lean Product Development, Agile Product Development, Lean Startup, and Design Thinking.

Keurig benefitted greatly from Roger's experience implementing Lean ideas in product development at two prior companies with varying degrees of success. Before adopting Rapid Learning Cycles, they first attempted to use an adapted form of Agile Software Development based on Scrum, combined with some principles from Roger's earlier work on the importance of leveraging prior knowledge to focus on NUDs. The next chapter will show why Lean and Agile practices help to accelerate innovation, and why they are not sufficient on their own to achieve High Velocity Innovation.

Your Next Actions

☐ Look for examples of external pull coming from your customers and markets: seasonality, trade shows, and budgeting cycles.

☐ Review communications about your company's strategy to see if it includes a strategic imperative for innovation.

☐ Review the list of innovation programs you created in Chapter 1 and list the ways that these innovation programs experienced pull. Then reflect on when the innovators had to push their ideas onto another group by selling them on the idea.

CHAPTER THREE

THE HIGH VELOCITY INNOVATION SYSTEM

In 2017, Agersens was named one of the world's top disruptive brands by *Marketing Week Magazine* because of its potential to replace traditional fences on farms. The company is a startup based in Melbourne, Australia, that sells the eShepherd—a GPS-enabled virtual herding collar with a cloud platform for automated livestock grazing control. This product could eventually eliminate the need for fencing, herding, and mustering on farms and rangeland stations. It requires in-depth knowledge of GPS, mapping technologies, Internet-of-Things (IoT) systems, and long-range radio communications in remote areas. Their first product was launched in May of 2018.

The agricultural technology industry sells products to a conservative market of farmers and land holders. If there's any doubt about the product's ability to work when it's launched, it's typically difficult to recover from such a setback and have a second chance to impress. Agersens developed the eShepherd in an area with challenging customers, challenging physical environments, and the need to build new IoT hardware alongside a complete system.

In this type of development program, the fast development cycles of Agile and Lean Startup break down. The team's early incubator taught Lean Startup, but their CTO, Chris Leigh-Lancaster, recognized that the methodology was insufficient to equip his team for the challenges in front of them. Their minimum viable product (MVP) took three months to develop, and that was just the basics to demonstrate virtual fencing; it was a Proof-of-Concept still a long way from a product that could be put on the market.

Chris subsequently used Rapid Learning Cycles and other elements of High Velocity Innovation to help his team develop the full eShepherd product and navigate the shift from a small startup team with a lot of external partners into a full internal development team. He said:

> Rapid Learning Cycles is the only thing we've come across that deal with the challenges we see in complex IoT projects with combined hardware/software development. To do a field test on animals takes a long time, so the whole idea of getting rapid feedback breaks down quickly. RLCs do a much better job of managing that.

If your company only makes software or services, then the combination of Agile and Lean Startup will achieve High Velocity Innovation. Agile's development practices mesh well with Lean Startup's emphasis on building MVPs then iterating rapidly by using customer feedback to improve their product/market fit. But if yours is a physical product requiring supply chains, production, and distribution, then they won't be enough on their own.

The focus of my work has been to find the methods that do accelerate innovation in these areas and others in which the assumptions of Agile and Lean Startup don't apply.

The Roots of the High Velocity Innovation System

This framework rests on my experience combining decades of research into the best ways to bring disruptive products and other large-scale innovations to life. Along the way, I've pulled in the practices that led to demonstrable improvements for my clients, and dropped the stuff that just didn't work. Figure 3.1 shows these influences.

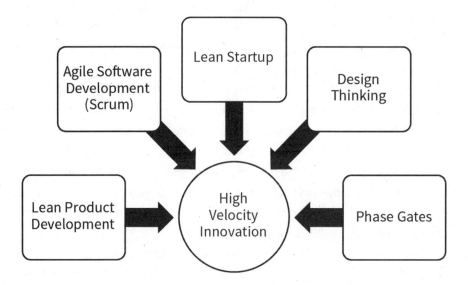

Figure 3.1: The roots of High Velocity Innovation.

Some of that work was done in the 2000s, when startup founders and mentors sought ways to make their fledgling firms more likely to succeed. Steve Blank and Eric Ries consolidated these lessons into the Lean Startup methodology. Meanwhile, Tim Brown, Tom Kelley, and David Kelley of IDEO pioneered a customer-centric approach to product design that put the customer first, which they called Design Thinking.

Blank and Reis built the Lean Startup on top of a framework constructed during the heady days of the first Internet boom, when software developers made the transition away from developing large systems for mainframe computers and boxed software for PCs. Instead, Internet technology gave developers the ability to make changes rapidly and release new versions more often with less cost and risk. Agile Software Development experts leveraged this new capability into practices that simultaneously improved the time lines, cost, and quality of software development. Others started to experiment with these practices for other types of products.

On the hardware side, product developers took inspiration from Toyota's product development and production systems. Toyota had been working since the end of World War II to eliminate waste, reduce time-to-market, and improve quality in its systems. The Lean Product Development movement sought to help other companies use these insights about how to run these processes efficiently.

Companies could take advantage of these methods because by the mid 1990s, most companies had a phase gate process inspired by Robert Cooper's research, as documented in *Winning With New Products*. Cooper described a Product Development Process broken down into phases, with clear gates between them to serve as management control points. Cooper built his work on top of much-maligned waterfall development, which was the first attempt to bring order from the chaos that predominated early software development work.

Today, companies that are serious about innovation often use an eclectic blend of Lean, Agile, and Design Thinking overlaid on a phase gate process that may have been designed for incremental product development. These methods work a lot better when innovation leaders understand how these methods create pull, and what behaviors they are pulling from the innovation teams, along with the areas in which these methods may push teams into beliefs and practices that hinder progress.

Innovation Methods Pull Good Work and Push Side Effects

The methods described previously are complementary; a team could use practices from all of them simultaneously. Many app and services teams that operate in a corporate environment use Lean Startup to help define and improve the app or service, especially at first. They use Design Thinking to come up with preliminary solutions for the user interface and industrial design. They run the program using Agile practices and improve their operational and delivery processes with Lean. They do all of this in the context of a phase gate process that controls the flow of money and resources within the company.

Any of these methods will deliver step changes in an innovation team's performance—if the team has the specific problem that the method was designed to solve. Each method also comes with unintended side effects. They all pull some good behaviors, but push some notions that can trip up an innovation team that is unaware of the pitfalls.

Lean Startup Pulls MVPs—and Pushes Premature Builds

Lean Startup begins with the belief that a startup is a grand experiment with a clear hypothesis to test: if a founder's company builds X product for Y customer using Z business model, he or she will create sufficient value for investors to ensure the company's survival, growth, and maturity. This idea was a breakthrough in the field of startup management. It has broad implications for how to move from idea to concept for every innovation team.

I will call that statement the Core Hypothesis, and every innovation under active development has one, whether it's explicit or not. The Core Hypothesis for Agersens's eShepherd could be written as:

> The eShepherd is a full virtual fencing solution from the collar to the app that eliminates the need for physical fences as it provides better information about the location of each member of a herd to increase production and lower costs so that we grow Agersens into profitability.

Embedded in that statement are some hypotheses that Chris's team needed to validate: that virtual fencing is possible, that it does eliminate the need for physical fences, that rangers do experience lower costs and higher productivity, and that the market potential is large enough to drive eventual profitable growth.

A startup team that follows this model will first seek to validate the Core Hypothesis by talking with customers about their needs and about the concept. Then the team will develop a "MVP—the product that has the minimum feature set necessary to meet a customer's minimum requirements to fulfill the need. This is also an experiment: what happens when customers use the product? Do they get the expected value? Based on that, does the team have a viable business? A successful MVP kicks off a series of iterative product releases to enhance and improve it, which can continue indefinitely in the app space.

Then each product release is an experiment to test a hypothesis around a specific change or addition to the MVP, with clearly defined measures and success criteria. This approach pulls rigorous design of experiments from teams to get clean results from their tests. If a hypothesis fails, the team runs another experiment. If the Core Hypothesis of the entire business proves to be wrong, teams can pivot to a new hypothesis, based on what they already learned. Reis encapsulated this into "Build–Measure–Learn," which is a vast improvement over the "Build–Test–Fix" cycles in which engineers get by default.

But what if it's not easy to build an MVP and then iterate on it quickly because lead times for suppliers, tooling, and distribution take too long? What if your product is competing for shelf space during set marketing windows? What if your product is seasonal, and therefore your customers and distribution partners only have bandwidth for one new product release per year? What if the riskiest parts of your Core Hypothesis are on the technology side versus the customer side? What if an established brand can't accept the risk of a MVP that's too skimpy to satisfy the current customer base?

In these spaces, the Lean Startup model breaks down because it emphasizes building products and getting them in front of customers as fast as possible. For some types of products, especially those that require large-scale production, a product build is not the fastest way to learn. For many physical products, rushing to build a product too early will slow down the team's progress toward a final product that delivers value because the product build isn't going to test the design in ways that validate their materials, production methods, or the user experience.

They may need to test how well a new material will handle being exposed to extremes of heat and cold before investing in too much design work. They may need to validate that a handle design is ergonomic before they buy an injection mold that will be difficult to change. They may need to prove that a formula for a cleaning product works better than competitors at lab scale, using standard tests, before they can go ahead with the packaging design, regulatory filings, and industrial-scale production that even a small market test requires.

Instead of "Build–Measure–Learn" these teams need "Design–Experiment–Capture" as shown in Figure 3.2. They need to design their learning activity or experiment with a clear hypothesis, run that experiment, and then capture their observations and results.

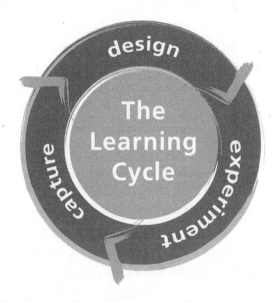

Figure 3.2: The Design–Experiment–Capture loop.

High Velocity Innovation requires a team to rigorously test its ideas in the fastest possible way. The team has to be clear about its Core Hypothesis, and needs to be open to lots of different paths to get to a final product. For Agersens, Rapid Learning Cycles encouraged their teams to find lots of ways to learn that don't require the long feedback loops of a full product release.

Design Thinking Pulls Customer Intimacy—and Pushes Reinvention

To understand customer needs that go beyond superficial surveys and focus groups, research has to begin with Design Thinking. These teams observe potential customers in the places where the product will be used. This helps to see opportunities that the customers cannot see and to build shared knowledge about a customer's journey as it is now, and as it will be with the new product. The focus is to make sure the team can identify the problem they will solve for their customers and what an ideal solution would be.

Then they get feedback from customers by iterating through rapid prototypes and presenting alternative solutions to give the users something to react against. The customer representative becomes a member of a collaborative team that seeks the best solution by trying out lots of different things as fast as possible. Rapid experimentation leads to rapid improvement, and increases the likelihood that the team will uncover something about the problem or the solution that no one else has seen. In combination with Lean Startup practices, it's a powerful way to build a startup.

Design Thinking is great for developing ideas and evaluating preliminary concepts. It's not so great at leveraging what the organization already knows. Teams are encouraged to start with a clean sheet of paper and use crude tools for conceptual prototyping that are not representative of the final product. The collaborative team structure creates a lot of creative energy, but if teams lack technical or business expertise, their creative solutions may be cost prohibitive to bring to market or violate the laws of physics. They also "reinvent" solutions for things that the company has already solved and create new solutions where they don't add value.

High Velocity Innovation encourages teams to use Design Thinking practices and tools to build deep knowledge about the needs of the customer and the specific problem that an innovation will solve.

At the same time, teams that start with a clean sheet for everything are teams that don't understand why their product is innovative, and therefore which areas they must invent versus which areas should be heavily leveraged from somewhere else. This means that a team using Design Thinking needs clear hypotheses for their prototype experiments so that they understand where they need innovative solutions, and where those innovations can be strengthened with existing knowledge.

Agile Pulls Flexibility—and Pushes Lack of Accountability

Agile Software Development grew out of the pain of trying to develop software for the Internet using practices that had been honed for large mainframe system development. By the late 1990s, it was clear that these practices didn't work well even on the large projects they were supposed to help. Studies in the 1990s showed failure rates, as measured by cancelled projects and applications no one used, at 80 percent. Meanwhile, some exciting things were happening on the Web.

At the time, Internet development was akin to the Wild West. The technology was immature and rapidly evolving. Customer behavior was a question mark; no one knew what it would take to get the average consumer to purchase stuff online. The infrastructure for payment processing, order fulfillment, shipment tracking, and returns was being constructed alongside the first sites that had a "Buy" button.

It was impossible to lock down requirements because no one knew what the requirements should be for things that had never been done before. It was impossible to lock down technical specifications because the rapid pace of evolution made them obsolete before they could get through their approval cycles. In this environment, traditional project plans and other planning documents have little value because they can't be kept up to date.

Agile Software Development emerged from a lot of experimentation about how to solve this problem so that developers could make progress in the face of such headwinds. The term "Agile" comes from the Agile Manifesto, a document that pulled these ideas together into a faster and more humane way of developing software.[2]

The roots of these practices grew from research done in the 1980s on software engineering best practices, but the methods came into their own when the cost-of-change for releasing software products became insignificant: teams could release new versions by publishing to a web-site or an app store. Today, some teams build new internal versions of their software every day, and the fastest teams can push changes out to users within two weeks.

The most common Agile method is Scrum, which organizes work into sprints, places tasks into backlogs, and then gives the product owner and the team power to choose tasks from the backlog that will be completed in a Sprint to deliver the most value in that Sprint. Each Sprint is a mini development project, with requirements, architecture, implementation, validation, and verification via a demo. There is no project schedule aside from the Sprint plan and the backlog, and little documentation except the code itself.

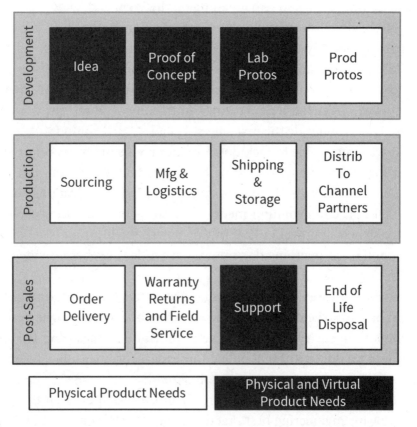

Figure 3.3: Differences between virtual and physical products.

But what if you can't release products without incurring significant costs? What if the work to deliver your innovation requires a series of steps to be completed in order, with complex chains of dependencies? What if you can't complete one full cycle of Design–Implement–Test in a reasonable Sprint? What if you work in a regulated industry where "no documentation" isn't an option?

In these spaces, the cost-of-change is much higher, as is the need to ensure that the right things get done in the right order by the right people. Innovation teams still need to be Agile to deal with the uncertainties that they face. They need to be more flexible and responsive to change. But practices drawn from Agile Software Development need heavy adaptation.

Chapter Six will introduce the Rapid Learning Cycles framework, an adaptation of Agile practices for environments with high cost-of-change. Chapter Seven will explain when to use pure Agile, when to use traditional Project Management methods, and when to use Rapid Learning Cycles to accelerate innovation. Agersens uses Agile for software development, during which the regular cadence and short feedback cycles allow the team to incorporate new feedback from customers and field trials on a Sprint-by-Sprint basis. On the hardware side, the feedback cycles are too long, and Rapid Learning Cycles is a better fit.

Lean Pulls Problem-Solving Discipline—and Pushes Rigidity

"Lean" in this context comes from the field of Operational Excellence. Most senior leaders have encountered it in the form of "Lean Manufacturing," a system for managing operations taken from studies of Toyota's production system. Its cousin, "Lean Product Development," derives from similar studies of Toyota's product development system.

Toyota achieved unsurpassed competitive advantage in the automotive industry through rigorous process discipline, from standardization and training through continuous improvement and constant pushes to achieve new levels of performance. Toyota's leaders learned they could meet rising expectations by eliminating waste in every process, from strategy deployment down to the smallest operation on the shop floor. The set of tools and practices that emerged from this research has broad applicability in transactional processes—those processes that are repeatable with short cycle times.

On the product development side, even Toyota recognized that process discipline wasn't the only thing teams needed. They built product development around the flow of knowledge creation, pulling learning earlier and pushing decisions later than their peers. They developed means to ensure that knowledge built in one program could be leveraged into future programs. They maximized the flow of knowledge across programs as platforms. As a result, in the 1990s, they were able to deliver new car models in half the time of their peers.

Their success is difficult to replicate. Unlike Lean Manufacturing, Lean Product Development has much lower adoption, even in the automotive industry. Product Development Process teams have spent a lot of time trying to build "leaner" processes without getting sustainable results. I contributed to this body of work from 2002 to 2012, before my client observations led me to pivot away from it. Ten years of trying was long enough to demonstrate that this model had some fundamental flaws.

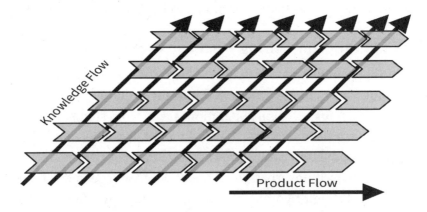

Figure 3.4: The flow of knowledge in product development.

But that doesn't mean this field is entirely without merit. Some of my clients' teams emphasized Lean practices around sharing knowledge, building platforms, pulling learning forward, and pushing decisions later, rather than waste elimination and process optimization. Those clients found that they could get their products to market faster.

This was the key that unlocked the value from Lean Product Development, as long as teams ignored almost everything else from Lean. In fact, High Velocity Innovation depends upon the ability to leverage as much knowledge as possible so that the innovation team can focus on the new, unique, and difficult aspects of their program.

Chris of Agersens says, "One of the key benefits is that it's allowed us to systematically build knowledge around the basic science within our product very quickly and then transfer that knowledge to new team members to shorten the time it takes to bring new employees up to speed." I'll share some practices for doing that in Chapter Eight.

Phase Gates Pull Accountability— and Push Decisions Too Early

In the 1990s, Robert Cooper's research showed that many companies struggled with releasing products because they didn't have a way to evaluate the health of a product development program while it was in flight.[1] Once a program started, it built momentum until it was impossible to stop—even if it was a bad idea.

Cooper recommended that organizations divide the work of product development into logical phases. Although every company's phase gate model uses different names, they typically include phrases like Concept Evaluation, Feasibility, Product Design, Process Design, Validation & Verification, and Launch. Each phase has a management control gate, and as a product moves through the process, the investment and commitment increases.

Theoretically, this allows management to decline product investments that are no longer good fits for the company or that are not working. In practice, these gates often become more like show-and-tell reviews.

Products still don't get killed, at least not at later phases, even if they no longer fit. Meanwhile, every functional group that needs something from a development team has used the gates to build checklists of "must do" deliverables like test plans, Failure Modes and Effects (FMEA) Analyses, frozen requirements and specifications, qualified suppliers, and tool vendors.

Phase Gate Product Development Process

Concept　　Design　　Execution　　Launch

Image 3.5: A simplified gate process.

In a well-functioning phase gate process, these stages are fluid, which allows teams to pull work early or delay deliverables that aren't complete as long as most of the work is done. But even when processes retain some flexibility, they encourage teams to make decisions too early in order to complete the deliverables checklist. The more innovative the program, the less likely it is that teams will have the knowledge they need to make good decisions early in a program. They are more likely to get bogged down later when their decisions don't work out as expected.

A keystone of High Velocity Innovation is the ability to make decisions at the right time, with the right people, and the best available knowledge. At the same time, phase gates should not be thrown out altogether. They need to be restored to their original purpose as management control points, including the ability to kill programs that are not working.

Startups don't normally have traditional phase gates, but they do have clear milestones to hit. They decide how good the product needs to be and what knowledge they need to build to hit the next milestone that opens up the next level of investment. Unlike most corporate innovation programs, the ability to hit these milestones are life-and-death for the company. Rapid Learning Cycles and the other practices of High Velocity Innovation have helped get them to their first product launch.

An Innovation System that Builds Velocity

The system I developed for High Velocity Innovation draws from all of the previously mentioned disciplines to the extent that their practices solve the problems that an innovation team typically has. Your innovation group needs the ability to use the practices that fit, and discard the ones that don't. High Velocity Innovation has implications for how an innovation team receives strategic direction, structures itself, manages its workflow and knowledge flow, chooses tools and systems, and measures itself.

If you've already gone all-in with Lean PD, Lean Startup, or Agile and it's not delivering what you hoped, then you're still better off than if you were doing product development the way you were before. Your teams have built some useful skills that need a little redirection so that they integrate into a system to accelerate innovation.

Your company builds innovation velocity by aligning your entire organization around the need for the specific innovations that will help the company realize its vision of the future, and putting in place the elements they need to do it. These elements include:

- **Strategic decisions:** Innovation teams need the organization's leaders to lead by establishing the company's strategic direction. They need a clear vision for the future of the company, strategic objectives to make the vision more concrete, and roadmaps that show the path from the present into the future. If a company can achieve all of this without expending any effort on innovation, then it probably will. But most companies find that they don't know everything and can't do everything they need in order to accomplish their vision. That's where the pull for innovation velocity starts.

- **Organizational and team structures:** People are accountable for achieving the company's strategic objectives, but they can only succeed if the organizational and team structures support them. Many authors recommend that innovation teams work in isolation from the core business to protect them from resistance.

However, in my experience, innovation teams thrive on balanced tension between a focus on delivering new capabilities through independence and a deep understanding of what the company can already do well through deep functional expertise. This tension builds innovation velocity by aligning functional groups with the need for innovation and giving them a stake in the successful execution of innovation.

- **Innovation Processes:** The primary way to build innovation velocity is to put an Innovation Process in place that reinforces the pull generated by the company's strategic objectives. Chapter Six will introduce Rapid Learning Cycles as a method for managing innovation programs that uses pull events to build urgency, rapid feedback, accountability, and alignment, even when a team is in the middle of a frustrating, uncertain period of development.

- **Platforms and extensible knowledge:** Platforms and extensible knowledge increase innovation velocity by expanding the possibilities for innovation. When an innovation team has access to the organization's knowledge, they have the raw materials for innovations that leverage the best of the company's resources into new solutions. Such innovations showcase the company's assets in unexpected ways. Even breakthrough and disruptive innovations benefit from the ability to access the company's collective wisdom so that the teams can focus on things that are new and different about the innovation without reinventing everything. A team moving with high velocity needs to leverage everything it can.

- **KPIs and results metrics:** Scorecards encourage people to score. The right metrics pull innovation from idea through execution by making results visible and clarifying what it means to win with innovation. The KPIs are how the organization knows that an Innovation Program is on track and functioning well. The results metrics are how the company knows that it is realizing results from its investments in innovation. They work together to measure innovation velocity and demonstrate that going faster has led to more growth.

Chris Leigh-Lancaster says,

For us, the proof is in the pudding. We've developed a product we put out in the field, and we've accelerated that into a product for commercial trials. We've had very little trouble with the hardware. Now we're able to rapidly iterate on the firmware and software because we've developed a strong hardware platform. If we were having trouble with the hardware, we wouldn't be able to move as quickly as we want on the software side.

The next section of the book will describe how you can accelerate new ideas by putting these pieces together into a system for High Velocity Innovation.

Your Next Actions

☐ If your company has a phase gate Product Development Process (PDP), look at the checklists for each phase, and reflect on when decisions need to be made in order to fulfill the checklist.

☐ If your company has had any experience with Agile, Lean, or Design Thinking, pull together a review to see how well these experiments have gone. Have they made the difference you hoped? Why or why not?

☐ List the elements of High Velocity Innovation and rate your organization's ability to generate pull, based on the reading you've done so far and the current state of your teams.

PART TWO

The Elements of High Velocity Innovation

CHAPTER FOUR

Strategy that Accelerates Innovation

Gallagher Group, Ltd., in New Zealand has innovation in its DNA. The company was started in the 1930s by Bill Gallagher, Sr. who wanted to keep his horse from using his car as a scratching post. He devised a simple circuit that would give off a mild shock if the horse rocked the car. Gallagher built a company around electric fencing. His son pushed the innovation boundaries into other animal management, fuel dispensing, and security solutions.

Today, Gallagher's leadership team manages a portfolio of award-winning products across three business units, with other strategic investments managed through Gallagher Ventures. Their track record of success was built on innovation. The company's history demands the development of novel solutions to customer challenges.

High Velocity Innovation starts with a strategy that demands it. If the first part of this book was compelling, then your company's strategy already has some pull or you see the potential for a strategy that could create this pull. This strategy doesn't have to be perfect or take months of analysis to perfect. It just needs to provide a clear direction.

Where does your company need innovation? Are you striving to be the innovation leader on the product? Or do you want more process innovation to drive down costs? Do you have a new business model or new markets you want to reach? Do you need to get better at identifying, acquiring, and integrating acquisitions? Where will your company's future growth come from?

The Minimum Viable Strategy

If your company lacks any strategy at all, then it's worth taking a few weeks (but probably not more than that) to put something together to give your teams a better place to start. You might even find that innovation is not a key part of your strategy going forward. But even the smallest businesses have a sense of the direction they want to go.

The process doesn't need to take a long time or a ton of analysis. Every corporate strategy, no matter how thoroughly researched, is a hypothesis to test and then adjust. Like anything with high uncertainty, it's best to explore quickly and fail fast than to get everything perfect from the beginning.

I'm not a strategy consultant. I help companies implement their strategies by removing the barriers to innovation. My perspective is from the innovation team that is tasked with fulfilling the company's strategic objectives for innovation. I'm not going to describe the process for developing a "good enough" strategy. There are a lot of good books out there about how to do strategy development, and I've listed a couple of my favorites in the "Further Reading" section.

Instead, I'll share what your innovation teams need from your company's strategy. From the perspective of your innovation teams, it's better to spend a short period of time to get something out there than it is to force them to wait while you analyze every possible angle. It's even worse to force them to innovate in a vacuum while you develop the "perfect" strategy, and then force them to abandon all that work when the new strategy gets published.

Here, I'll describe the role that strategy plays in accelerating innovation, and the elements that strengthen this pull. You'll probably find that your company's current business, product, and operational strategies have some gaps to close. You can close those gaps as you work to put the other elements of High Velocity Innovation in place. When the entire system is ready, you're capable of generating the pull you need to make the most of it.

Strategy Pulls Ideas that Fit

When I started thinking about buying a Mini Cooper, all of a sudden I saw Mini Coopers all around town. They were there in the flow of traffic the entire time, but my perceptual filter wasn't tuned to see them.

Prior to that, I owned a Toyota Prius and I used to see them all over town, even though they were rare at the time. But hybrid cars need to be driven often to keep the batteries healthy. As my travel schedule increased, the car sat idle for too long, and the batteries stopped working well. I realized this technology was a poor fit for me. Now hybrid cars don't pass through my filters even though they are much more common today than when I owned one.

Good strategy works the same way: it tunes your organization's perceptual filters so that the good ideas you need come to the surface, and the ones you don't fade into the background. The good ideas build support, capture management attention, and attract resources. The poor ideas get recognized faster and deprioritized sooner. That saves everyone a lot of time to accelerate the good ones.

What is a good strategy to pull innovation? One that is specific, pragmatic, and well-communicated.

Specificity Is More Important than Vision

This strategy doesn't have to be world-changing or visionary. A lot of visionary leaders fail because their teams can't execute without the missing details, as more pragmatic peers build sustainable growth. Visions are what the company intends to become; strategic plans define how the company will get there. Visions need the type of details that come out of a strategic plan to become actionable.

This means that it should be easy to see what is in alignment with the strategy and what is not in alignment with the strategy. One good test of the strategy is to throw up some wild ideas to see if they fit in with the strategy or not. If the strategy calls for growth by developing lower-cost products for emerging markets, then it's probably not in scope to invest in a premium product for North America.

Few companies have the resources to do everything they could do, and this means that the leaders have to choose or the organization will choose for them. If you overload your teams with too many things, they will decide how to prioritize their time. In the absence of good direction from leadership, they tend to choose the easiest and fastest things to do, and they will probably not choose the same things to move forward first.

Specificity gives you the power to establish focus and alignment, two elements that are essential for accelerating innovation. Here are some of the details that help teams achieve this:

- **What the company will do:** At a fundamental level, does the company make a specific kind of product, develop lots of products to meet the needs of a given market, or encourage adoption of a specific technology into lots of application spaces that generate products?

- **Where it will play:** What markets, regions, and product categories will be the company's focus? Out of all the people who could be customers, which ones will receive the company's attention? Out of all the things a company could do for them, what will it do?

- **Where it will not play:** Where is it acceptable for the company to meet a customer's threshold expectation in order to compete elsewhere? Some corporate strategies focus on price; others focus on quality and features. Where is "good enough" acceptable and where is excellence required?

- **How it will win:** What the company leaders perceive the company's competitive advantage to be today and what they believe it could become in the future.

Strategies with specificity are much easier to treat as the hypotheses that they are rather than a set of vague visionary statements. Figure 4.1 has the fundamental questions that should have answers in your "good-enough" strategy. These answers help your teams understand what innovation your company needs from them. It's easier to know what success looks like, and therefore easier to find Key Performance Indicators (KPIs) that can provide early validations of success or warnings of failure.

Figure 4.1: The questions an innovation strategy should answer.

Gallagher's entire strategy is built around the areas in which they have a unique contribution to make through innovation. Their category strategies make this specific to the needs of the category business, and category roadmaps flow the strategies into concrete programs.

When your teams can draw a direct line from the reality that they see on the ground to these specific strategy elements and the future direction of the company, you have a pragmatic strategy that will pull ideas.

Pragmatic Strategy Can Lead to Breakthrough

The strategy needs to be grounded in real-world experiences, observations, and information as much as possible because it must be credible and explainable to the company's stakeholders (including its employees). Especially for the people who are attracted to engineering and science, it's important to know why, and that "why" needs to make sense so that they can internalize the logic. When they have that ability to internalize the strategy, they are more likely to develop the ideas that will lead to breakthroughs in the areas most important to the company.

"Pragmatic" doesn't have to mean boring or lacking ambition. You could have identified a great opportunity that requires a tremendous amount of innovation to achieve. You could be facing a competitive threat that will demand new ways of doing business if your company is going to thrive as markets change.

The strategy doesn't have even have to call for innovation leadership. There is a lot of room for innovation in being a fast follower by developing the capability to learn quickly from the leaders. Teams then execute quickly on a product that's better because it fixes the mistakes and capitalizes on the missed opportunities in the leaders' products. Some of the work I've done to help teams develop low-cost alternatives has been some of the most interesting, challenging innovation work I've ever done.

In fact, when you pull cost out of a program, it can lead to breakthrough innovations that create competitive advantage, which is hard for others to copy. This is the strategy that allowed Toyota and other Japanese car manufacturers to establish strong positions in the worldwide auto industry. Ford, GM, and others spent years studying what Toyota had done, copying what they could extract from suppliers and from the information Toyota was willing to share.

But Toyota created a culture of process innovation that acted at every level to eliminate waste and lower costs, because the strategic need for process innovation was clear from the top-level strategy down to shop floor objectives. This is much harder to copy, and would have been impossible without a specific, pragmatic strategy that could sort out the good ideas from the distractions.

Gallagher's primary markets are some of the most conservative in the world: farmers, government agencies, and correctional facilities. These are not customers who purchase the latest innovation for the sake of owning it. Everything Gallagher does has to start with customer and business value.

Clear Strategy Eliminates Distractions

If your company perceives the need for any type of innovation (product, process, business model, operations) as part of its strategy, then that needs to be communicated to the people who will generate these ideas—which could be anyone in the company. Because it defines the playing field on which new ideas will be tested, it can't be posted in the executive office where no one can see it. It can't generate pull if only a few people understand it.

Although I saw lots of companies accelerate innovation in the absence of a clear strategy by building pull in other ways, the companies that have done the best are the ones whose teams had internalized the corporate strategy and interpreted it for their program. They have an easier time capturing leaders' attention for resources and major decisions.

But clarity is easier to talk about at an executive level than it is to achieve on the ground.

Clarity at a Strategic Level Is Hard to Achieve

Often leaders have access to much more information about the company's current state and future direction, market and business trends, and investor expectations than their employees. That can make some strategic decisions incomprehensible to the rank-and-file who lack this context. Yet without this clarity, people wander around lost in a foggy atmosphere that kills any impulses toward innovation.

This is especially true if the strategy requires major restructuring; that can cause people to hunker down into their current roles and resist change even more fiercely. During major reorganizations, people use up their creative energy on figuring out how to get their work done without the visible and invisible structures that supported them in the past. Sometimes such drastic measures are necessary, but leaders need to be mindful of the impact that restructuring has on a company's ability to execute, and the opportunity cost of lost time, energy, and focus.

If the strategy is poorly communicated, changing too often, or creating unnecessary turmoil, innovation can come to a standstill. Innovation is uncertain enough without the constant disruption caused by a leadership team's inability to focus on a few clear objectives for more than a few months. Teams operating in spaces of high instability need leaders to be resolute about their strategic decisions; this creates a zone of stability the team can draw upon to cope.

Innovation thrives in an atmosphere with strategic objectives that point toward the types of innovation that the company needs to build sustainable growth, and a commitment to give the strategy time to prove itself. When leaders can communicate the company's strategic objectives with specificity, pragmatism, and clarity, teams and individuals will be prepared to recognize and support the ideas that will lead to the innovative solutions that will deliver these objectives.

Communicating Strategic Decisions with Clarity

When was the last time you attended a "strategic update" for your company? If there are more than 250 people inside the company, most of your teams receive the information from this update third-hand. Chances are, someone not directly involved in crafting the strategy presented a bunch of slides that were handed down from above, without fully understanding what was supposed to be said.

It's bad enough if the strategic goals are all incremental and numbers-driven. In terms of innovation goals, it's not nearly enough to communicate what your teams need to know to make them successful. Communication needs to be multi-modal and multi-sensory in order to build strong alignment, and team objectives must flow from the strategy in a way that makes sense to the team.

Customer-Centric Visions and the Customer's Journey

The overall goal of the strategy needs to be expressed in customer-centric terms. This is one element that every person at every level needs to understand viscerally. The developers must see what needs to be done from a customer's perspective. The customer is not always right, and often the customer can't tell the developers what they need to know. However, the developers don't have any basis for evaluating that if they don't know who their customer is.

When it comes to innovation, customer profiles and avatars are great ways to build alignment around who the customer is and what he or she needs. This is especially important for new customers. Chances are, your teams already have a good handle on the existing customers; at the very least, they have an instinctive grasp of what they need. They need this same deep understanding for new customers.

During the Innovation Program, the teams need to go out and get inside the customers' experiences. But if you make a strategic decision to go down a particular road with specific customers, then some of that prep work should have enabled you to paint this picture in broad outlines.

Stories to Build Bridges from the Past to the Future

Companies, even startups, have history. Some people in your company will be more attached to that history than others, but everyone needs to know how to get from where you are now to where you want to be.

Stories work because they get behind the logic of what you do to connect with people emotionally. They provide the bigger "why" behind the strategy to show how your company will create value, whatever that value is. They align actions with shared beliefs, especially around the company's aspirations.

If you make any consumer product, especially one that focuses on health, safety, or enjoyment, telling stories is how you build an emotional connection with your customers. If you make an industrial product, this is how you connect people to your direct consumers and to your ultimate consumers. These stories paint a multidimensional picture that shows how lives will change as a result of your product. If you're in a business like green energy or medical devices, you have a compelling story to tell. But even the most prosaic consumer product has a reason why your consumers will buy it, and if you can make that picture clear, it generates more pull.

For other companies, the better story may be the company itself. You can base a story around your company's journey from startup to maturity. You can base it around the need to beat back a competitive threat, or the possibilities of expanding into a new market. You can talk about the future company you want to build for your investors, employees, and community. You may have stories from the early days of the company that explain why your company has such a strong brand. You may have stories of how you were able to survive economic downturns and major business disruptions. If you can tie these stories to your company's strategic goals, you build a bridge from the current state to the future.

Gallagher has eighty years' worth of stories, starting with the story of Bill Gallagher Sr. and his horse, to transmit the DNA of innovation from experienced team members to new ones. The company shares its stories with the media, on its website, and with all of its employees. People associated with Gallagher know that they have to be innovative because they have a legacy to live up to.

Visual Models and Infographics

If stories explain "why," visual models and infographics explain "what and how" at a strategic level. They clarify the logical relationships behind your decisions. They help others see the data the same way that you do. They align actions and beliefs with a shared understanding of the current reality.

Leaders need to be careful with these models, especially if they have been developed by a consulting firm and not the company leaders. They are still subject to misinterpretation because the people on the receiving end don't have all the background information that went into them. Sometimes the effort spent to make them look pretty detract from their clarity, and sometimes the effort to cram too much information into them blurs the most important relationships.

When carefully thought out and combined with stories and details, these models align the pictures the executives have in their minds with the pictures that their teams get when people hear about the strategies for the first time. That's especially true if the strategy uses the focusing power of cascading objectives.

Cascading Objectives with Strategic Alignment

When your teams can draw a straight line from the strategy back to them, it becomes real. Cascading objectives define how a specific group within the company will contribute to the fulfillment of the strategy. They don't need to have an objective for every strategy, however, they do need to know how they will make a meaningful contribution beyond running the current operation. For the group responsible for production, it could be to increase efficiency in new production lines to free up capital. Figures 4.2 and 4.3 show how strategic objectives can cascade all the way down to the level of the individual innovator.

The objective of an innovation team is to contribute innovation. The team's objective should state what type of innovation the team is pursuing without specifying the innovation itself. For example, if your company decides to move into the Latin American market, let the team tasked with that effort understand what the opportunities are and where your products and business processes need to be adapted to fit.

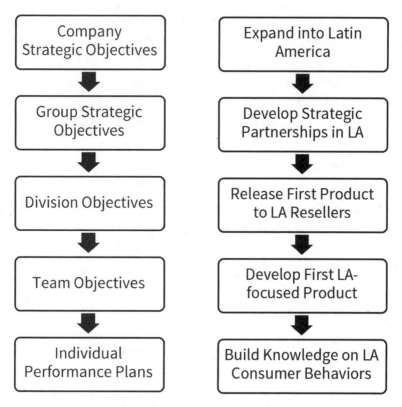

Figure 4.2 (left): How strategic objectives cascade down an organization.
Figure 4.3 (right): An example of cascading objectives.

The danger is that the exercise of defining cascading objectives can be subject to the same overanalysis delays that slow down the strategy. If it takes a whole quarter for the strategy to move from the executive suite to the labs, that's too long. Like most things in the innovation world, this process goes a lot faster when it's tied to a short deadline.

Roadmaps and Time lines

The final strategic element of successful innovation cascades the company's general strategy over the next several years into specific roadmaps and time lines for innovation. A roadmap places a group's objectives into a time line, showing how the accomplishment of one goal leads to the next. For innovation teams, roadmaps provide the initial targets for when an innovation will be delivered to the business.

Figure 4.4 shows how these roadmaps flow into each other and into innovation programs. The strategic plan informs technology and Product Roadmaps. That guides the leadership team as they manage their research and product portfolios of programs. Program Charters pull from these documents to define the Innovation Program.

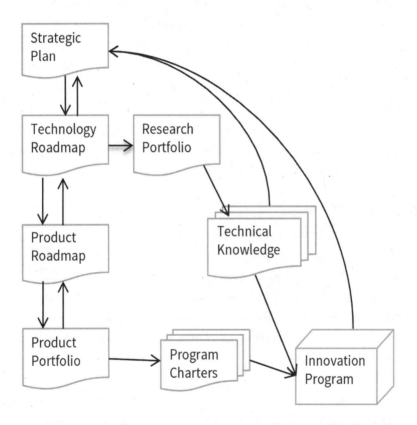

Figure 4.4: How strategies and roadmaps guide innovation programs.

Some companies, especially those that sell into consumer markets, have sophisticated roadmaps that show how products and platforms will be released in sync with market needs. From my time at HP and other consumer companies, I know that the holidays are a major selling season for many consumer products. Consumers look for new products and retailers have a full promotional season to populate with compelling offers. Such companies often have three- or five-year roadmaps showing products for each selling season by category and segment. A few go beyond that to show the new technologies, features, and design elements that will be released along with each product.

I have not seen these roadmaps as often in companies that sell to other businesses or in markets without such strong seasonality. But the roadmaps help generate internal pull, especially if they are tied to something that has external pull, like a major customer's budgeting cycle. Figure 4.5 on the opposite page is an example of a Product Roadmap for a company that makes coatings like paint and scratch protection for the automotive industry.

Gallagher has technology roadmaps and category roadmaps to turn innovation strategies into time lines. They pull innovation by giving invention a deadline.

Core Hypotheses

The Core Hypothesis is the glue that connects an innovation team to the strategy, and the primary way that a company's strategic direction gets validation. This one-sentence statement encapsulates the strategic intent for the product's technology, customer value, and business value. Figure 4.6 shows the three dimensions of the Core Hypothesis.

You'll see this Core Hypothesis come up repeatedly throughout this part of the book because it prevents so much wasted time due to misunderstandings, misalignments, or hidden disagreements. Unlike the other documents discussed previously, the team develops the Core Hypothesis for its own program. The process of creating it is good validation of how well a strategy has been communicated. If they struggle or they're off base, this is where it shows up first.

The process of writing the Core Hypothesis helps teams internalize the strategy and the need for innovation that leadership has tried to communicate with clarity and specificity. Unlike product vision or mission

Five Year Product Roadmap Fall 2020 – Spring 2025									Heisenberg Specialty Chemicals Car Exterior Finishes Division	
Product Family	Fall 2020	Spring 2021	Fall 2021	Spring 2022	Fall 2022	Spring 2023	Fall 2023	Spring 2024	Fall 2024	Spring 2025
OEM Coatings – two years from 1st vehicle	HSC200 w better scratch resist.		HSC220 w self healing coating		HSC500 Self Cleaning Paint		HSC500 in expand color range		HSC700 Thermo-chrome	
Aftermarket Coatings – for NAPA, AutoZone, etc.		ProtectIt Self Cleaning Spray		FixIt Home Scratch Removal Coating		FixIt2 with less dry time		SunOut UVCoat at home use		SunOut2 UVCoat w easier applic.
Fleet Solutions – professional applications	EcoCoat Self Cleaning Spray		FixItPro Scratch Removal Coating		EcoCoat 2 Self Cleaning Spray		UVCoat UV Reflect Coating		UVCoat2 w easier applic.	

Figure 4.5: A product roadmap for a specialty coatings company.

statements, this type of statement encourages teams to understand the assumptions that underlie the Core Hypothesis, and to seek ways to validate it.

Figure 4.6: The Core Hypothesis.

Strategy Pulls a Culture of Innovation

After building a strategy, it's not only natural to reflect on the organization's ability to deliver on that strategy, but also wonder if there is anything inherent about the company that will help or hinder it. As companies mature, the freewheeling culture that defines the startup gives way to those who appreciate process discipline, policies, and procedures because that's what a mature company needs for consistency. Then these mature companies wonder how to get back the spirit of innovation that characterized their early days.

My experience shows that culture is built from a company's beliefs about itself, which are manifested in their leaders' and employees' day-to-day actions and decisions. This is why it's not enough to have a vision. The strategy turns the vision into concrete goals; communicating and cascading the strategy makes it actionable. Holding people accountable for achieving their strategic objectives brings it to life.

Companies have poured millions of dollars into culture change efforts to make their people embrace innovation, change, and ambiguity rather than be stuck in the past. But the evidence shows few successes for all the effort, time, and money spent. I think this is because it doesn't address the root causes of the problem: the lack of pull for innovation in the strategy, the failure to communicate and reinforce the company's most important strategic goals, and the lack of accountability for achieving the strategy.

Gallagher is an example of a company that never lost that "spark" of innovation after eighty years. They never stopped demanding innovation from their people and continued to bring in outside ideas to help them. Gallagher began using Lean Product Development ideas in the late 2000s and then transitioned to Rapid Learning Cycles in 2016. Today, they have the elements of High Velocity Innovation. As a result, they have been able to deliver innovations faster.

Successful Innovation Builds a Culture of Innovation

For innovation in particular, cultural change doesn't lead to more innovation. Cultural change is a push; innovation thrives on pull. Cultural change implies that something is wrong with your employees; High Velocity Innovation starts with changing as an innovation leader by changing the expectations you have for your team as communicated through their strategy, plans, and metrics.

If you haven't asked for innovation, you need to give people fair warning that the nature of the game they're playing is about to change; some people won't understand, some will resist, and some may even try to sabotage. Those people can and should find other places where they feel more comfortable.

But don't listen to people who tell you this is going to take years of effort or "It's a journey." That saps all the life out of the exciting work you have ahead of you. Bill Gallagher Sr. didn't ask anyone's permission to electrify his car.

Your Next Actions

☐ If you're in a leadership role, use the questions in Figure 4.1 to evaluate the health of your strategy. What's strong? What could be strengthened? What's missing?

☐ No matter where you are in the organization, reflect on how your company's strategy and communications concerning its strategic decisions generate pull for innovation now, and how that pull can be strengthened.

☐ Work with your team to build a Core Hypothesis for the program in which you spend most of your time today. What is its connection to your company strategy?

CHAPTER FIVE

THE RAPID INNOVATION TEAM

Constellium develops and manufactures high-value aluminum products from alloy to finishing, focusing on the aerospace, automotive, and packaging markets. In 2016, the company's advanced innovation team recognized an opportunity to take advantage of cheap sensors and cloud technology to achieve greater knowledge and control over the manufacturing process, a project they called "Big Data."

People don't always think about such initiatives as "innovation" because most of the work isn't visible outside the company. But Constellium is extremely focused on the consistency of its fabrication processes, so that companies like Airbus can count on the quality and performance of the alloys and parts it produces. Introducing more intelligence and transparency into those processes would contribute to building Constellium's sustainable, difficult-to-copy competitive edge.

Constellium's Technology Development group has a small, dedicated innovation team combining high-performing R&D researchers, new hires bringing in new skills, and a manager with both technical expertise and strong connections across Constellium's businesses. Only small investigations are done fully inside the team.

For Big Data, the Proof–of–Concept needed to run inside a production facility to answer the most important questions. The Innovation Program Leader needed to partner with Information Technology and Production in order to run even small experiments.

Innovation Thrives on Collaboration

A skunkworks team of dedicated and isolated innovators would have never gotten such a complex program off the ground, because the program faces all the same resistances as business model or product innovation. In addition, extensive changes to the production lines have implications for environmental, health, and safety concerns that make the company's manufacturing and IT leaders especially risk averse. The Operations leaders need to embrace this change and involve them from the beginning, acknowledging their deep expertise while pulling them into the future.

Innovation Is Everyone's Responsibility

In Chapter 1, I mentioned that a company cannot offload responsibility for innovation to dedicated teams. Although that may be more comfortable for everyone, it reinforces the idea that the organization cannot innovate, and it limits the kinds of innovations that a company can explore. If building innovation teams with an isolated brand new staff worked, then such teams would have many more demonstrated successes.

When a company has strategic alignment around the need for innovation, pulling people out of functional groups for innovation programs reinforces the need for innovation across the company. Those people who are charged with running the current business receive encouragement and reinforcement for implementing innovative improvements. The members of the company who are least comfortable with new ideas can't hide from them, and so they will either get more comfortable or make their own decision to find a more comfortable place.

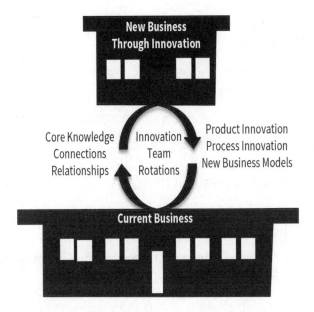

Figure 5.1: Innovation rotations pull in experienced people and core knowledge for actionable innovation.

Figure 5.1 shows the benefits of rotating people on and off of innovation teams. The teams benefit from core knowledge and connections, while the business gets more actionable innovation.

A healthy innovation team is structured by pulling members from within the organization. Some team members may be dedicated to innovation, but they are not isolated from their peers who work on the current business. Others may only work on an innovation team 25 percent of the time to perform specific tasks.

When innovation is everyone's responsibility, it's easier to pull people together from different functional groups so that the innovation team has the skills, knowledge, and organizational support to succeed.

Productive Innovation Teams Are Cross-Functional and Connected

Innovation is one of the most cross-functional activities an organization can do. Delivering a new product to market, designing a new business model, or reinventing the company's approach to production and distribution requires people who can:

- Recognize and characterize the market opportunity and strategic implications (Marketing).

- Develop Proof–of–Concepts and characterize the technical risks and opportunities (Engineering/Research).

- Analyze the expected pay-offs and investments required to bring the idea to fruition (Finance).

- Ensure teams understand freedom-to-operate and protect new ideas (Legal).

- Integrate the new idea into the company's existing systems for production and distribution (Operations).

Most people think about this idea in the context of a company that's organized into functional groups, but the same principle applies to other types of organizations, such as groups organized by product line or market.

Pull Innovation Team Members from the High Performers

The innovation team members stay connected to the core business, which creates healthy tension between the needs of the functions and the needs of the Innovation Program. When that tension is reinforced with urgency and accountability for delivering innovation, teams go faster. As Figure 5.2 shows, the ability to build strong functional expertise supports winning innovation.

Figure 5.2: Every innovation organization must balance functional teams and innovation teams.

Aside from Innovation Program Leaders and a handful of other specialists, most of these people can be given an Innovation Program as an assignment rather than a new job. This reinforces the idea that the company is innovative and that innovation is everyone's responsibility. The innovation team's peers get to see innovations come to life, which gives them opportunities to help and encourages them to be more innovative themselves.

At Constellium, Innovation Manager Ravi Shahani built a cross-functional team from the beginning for Big Data. Early engagement with IT and production teams made it easier to get permission to run experiments with a live production line. This relationship has paid off in other ways, too. For example, the innovation team makes an effort to shorten the time it takes for small-scale prototypes of new alloys via new ways of working with Production on these trials. That will increase innovation velocity for all of Constellium's programs.

When functional leaders maintain close relationships with members of their staff who have been assigned to support innovation teams, those leaders have a stake in the innovation team's success. Figure 5.3 shows that the organizations engaged in such work have an inherent matrix organization, whether they recognize it or not.

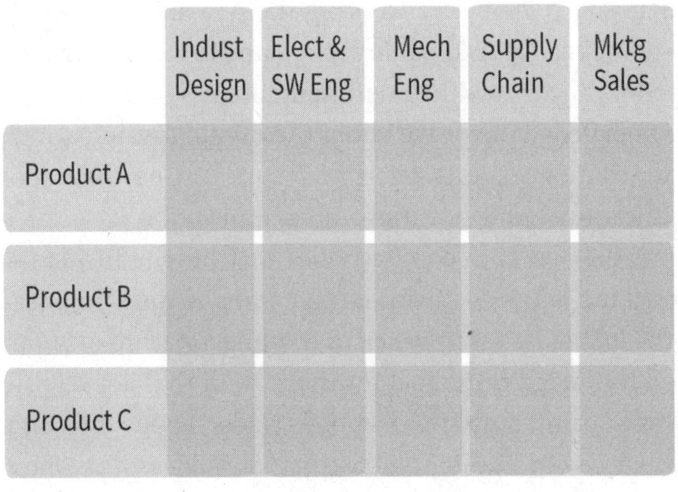

	Indust Design	Elect & SW Eng	Mech Eng	Supply Chain	Mktg Sales
Product A					
Product B					
Product C					

Figure 5.3: New product development is inherently matrixed.

When innovation team members maintain connections with their peers who are running the current business, they build and strengthen relationships they'll need when the innovation moves from investigation to execution. Good innovation team members recognize that for their ideas to be fully realized, they'll need to bring their peers along with them, especially if those peers want to put their heads down and run the current business.

Good Innovation Team Members Are Entrepreneurial

Successful entrepreneurs recognize early that they can't do everything themselves and that the world is not waiting for their new ideas. Therefore, they need the ability to build relationships with partners and potential customers. Entrepreneurs also need to be able to recognize opportunities, test them out, and then capitalize on the opportunities that are most promising. Without these abilities, a startup founder is more likely to become a failed entrepreneur that builds products that no customer wants, and that no investor will fund.

The best innovation team members have the ability to explore new ideas without becoming so attached to them that they don't see the flaws. They can draw other people into these explorations so that functional partners share the desire to bring the new ideas to life. They have a healthy tolerance for risk, while at the same time looking for opportunities to reduce the risk with experimentation.

The knowledge they have about the existing systems and structures, which innovation experts often discount, can be their most valuable contribution toward innovation. If an innovation is so far outside the company's defined core competencies that no one inside the company can contribute any value, why is the company investing in the innovation in the first place (as opposed to funding a startup or spinning it off)?

This knowledge is the fuel for innovation that delivers strategic value. When a team combines deep knowledge about the company's core competencies with the ability to explore new ideas, they have what they need to deliver High Velocity Innovation.

At Constellium, Ravi's small team of entrepreneurial innovators explore a handful of carefully vetted ideas around the product and process, including the development process. They work in a space that's just a few steps away from the main prototype testing lab. They have access to Constellium's experiences that goes back decades and people who have deep expertise. Although Ravi's team is dedicated to early-stage innovation, they are not isolated from the rest of the company.

Not everyone has these abilities to the same degree, and some organizations encourage these abilities better than others. At the same time, it's a mistake to write off an entire organization as "not capable of innovation" because they haven't delivered any visible innovations lately or seem to suppress new ideas. If the current business is successful, there are people who learned how to make the most of it. If it's struggling, there are people who learned how to get things done in spite of the challenges.

In fact, the people who are best at running the current business are exactly the ones needed for an Innovation Program because they have the ability to think like entrepreneurs when doing their own work. A person who has learned how to work effectively within a broken system is often the best person to help replace it. It takes good entrepreneurial skills to get even small ideas implemented in a risk-averse organization. Often, such people just need a good coach to help them master the specific skills that innovation teams need.

The Best Innovation Program Leaders Are Good Coaches

An Innovation Program Leader's primary responsibility is to build a team that can pull innovation through all the resistance and struggles it takes to bring an innovation to life. Although team members can and usually should come from the current business, running an Innovation Program is entirely different from running the current business or even running an incremental product development program.

When innovation is a shared responsibility, innovation team members need a leader who can help them make the transition from working inside the current business to working on something new. An Innovation Program Leader needs to be able to:

- Align the team, sponsors, and stakeholders around the vision for the Innovation Program and help them sustain that alignment as the vision shifts to accommodate new information.

- Coach the innovation team as they identify new ideas, evaluate them, and investigate them, which will require the team to learn new skills and use their existing skills in new ways.

- Build strong working relationships with the program's sponsors and other stakeholders.

- Guide the team, sponsors, and other decision makers as they evaluate risk versus reward for programs with high uncertainties.

- Use the right tools to manage the program, based on the phase the program is in.

The Innovation Program Leader is the "CEO" of the innovation team, responsible for making decisions that will have long-term implications for the company. At the same time, running an Innovation Program inside an established company is not like founding a startup. The Innovation Program Leader also needs to understand how the company works as a whole, so he or she can make the most of the opportunities and minimize the challenges.

The most important aspect of this role is the ability to coach the innovation team as they work through their challenges. If the innovation team members come from the current business, they will have experience with making decisions that make the most of the company's current systems.

This knowledge can provide the fuel for innovative thinking about the future, but they need to use tools that help them look at what they already know from different perspectives. This is where Design Thinking activities, creativity exercises, and design blitzes can help the team develop and evaluate a lot of ideas quickly to fulfill a strategic imperative, and then bring the best ones to maturity as concepts.

The Innovation Program Leader is the internal expert on how and when to use these tools. He or she sets new expectations for the team, and then provides support to help fulfill them. Depending on the innovation focus, this might include organizing a customer visit for observation, ensuring that the team is using good scientific methods to design experiments, leading the team through a creative exercise, or helping them prepare recommendations for a decision meeting with stakeholders.

This person can come from a variety of backgrounds, with some caveats. If a new idea requires substantial technical development, the person should have a strong technical background so he or she has credibility with the technical functions. If a new idea requires developing a new market, then strong marketing skills will be required.

In a technology company, the best person for the job has an engineering or scientific background but has spent time in another business area. This well-rounded experience positions the Innovation Program Leader to address the full range of challenges. It prepares the Innovation Program Leader to maintain visibility and focus on innovation from leadership in the midst of running the current business, with the help of the Innovation Sponsor.

Innovation Sponsors Keep the Innovation Flame Burning

Innovation programs need strong sponsorship if they're going to achieve high velocity, and many die because they don't have good visibility or support from leadership. This is a natural consequence of the short-term focus on quarterly profits, which is part of corporate culture. If leaders do nothing to protect innovation from the current business, the current business will always win, even if innovation is desperately needed for the company's long-term future.

The best protection against this is a strong, executive-level sponsor who believes deeply in the need for High Velocity Innovation. This person has a compelling need for innovation that arises from the company's strategy for the business. The sponsor needs to be high enough in the organization to approve requests for funding and resources without additional sign-offs and also have sufficient budget authority to establish a protected pool of funds to support innovation that others cannot touch. The Innovation Program Leader needs to be in the sponsor's organization, either reporting directly to the sponsor or to a manager one level down who also has innovation as a key performance objective.

This sponsor will:

- Represent the Innovation Program at the executive level, especially when the needs of the current business directly compete.

- Establish a protected funding pool that innovation teams can use to support their work.

- Build alliances with functional managers who will contribute innovation team members and other resources.

- Ensure that the Innovation Program is visible all the way to the top of the organization, with appropriate expectations, goals, and metrics.

- Hold the Innovation Program Leader and the innovation team accountable for using good methods that support High Velocity Innovation.

At a small company, the Innovation Sponsor should probably be the CEO or COO, with the Innovation Program Leader reporting directly to executive staff. At a larger company organized by division, the division's General Manager makes the most effective sponsor.

At a large functionally organized company, the best sponsor is usually the Line Manager responsible for delivering the strategic objective that requires innovation, such as the CTO, VP of R&D, or VP of Marketing. Large companies may also have enough Innovation Program Leaders to organize them into a functional group, but the Innovation Sponsors still need to come from the business rather than the Innovation function. It's too easy to sideline someone whose only responsibility is to deliver innovation, and it's too easy for dedicated Innovation Managers to forget that they need to pull innovation—not push it.

Sponsors interact with the team at key points in the Innovation Process: Kickoff Events to establish the team, events at which important decisions will be made, and the decision gates that determine whether a company will invest further in a specific idea. A sponsor should never go more than a quarter without some significant interaction with an innovation team. However, regular monthly or weekly reports take away the Innovation Program Leader's time and attention from other work. The specific ways a sponsor interacts with a team will depend upon the type of innovation team that he or she is sponsoring.

Team Structure for High Velocity Innovation

Innovation teams run the gamut from fully dedicated individuals in an innovation functional group to ad hoc teams put together to investigate specific ideas. An effective team structure has the following characteristics:

- Allows the team to view the company's core competencies from a perspective outside traditional organizational norms.
- Pulls knowledge from the organization into the innovation team, without restricting how that knowledge can be used.
- Provides for a smooth transition from Exploration to Investigation to Execution, with minimal knowledge leakage through handoffs.

Given these needs, it's easy to see why a dedicated innovation team make the most sense, as that creates an open space that should foster creativity. But dedicated innovation teams whose members leave their existing jobs (or come from outside the company) don't have the connections they need to execute successfully without a lot of pushing.

Innovation teams go faster if they are dedicated, but only for a specific period of time (perhaps six months). The deadline provides a clear end point when the team is expected to have some answers, and a time when team members' functional managers know that their people will be able to be redeployed back to the current business. If the Innovation

Program shows promising results, the team can go back to their normal roles and know that they'll continue to drive the innovation into execution, with support from their peers.

As an idea moves toward execution, the team needs to stay with the idea. They are the ones who went on the first customer visits that sparked the idea, and they are the ones who built the first prototypes and overcame the challenges. They are the experts on the knowledge that's been built about the idea so far, so they are the ones who should be primarily responsible for bringing it to life. As an innovation moves into execution, the team will grow to a full team. These new team members need the original team to help them get up to speed quickly on the vision for the product, avoid reworking issues that have already been closed, and dealing with the new information that continues to come even after launch on innovation programs.

Constellium's innovation programs incubated Big Data for two years before they had a good Proof-of-Concept and knew what it would take to fully realize the potential of this concept. The Production and IT teams stayed on the journey with the program. When it came time for executive leadership to approve a large investment in Big Data's next phase, the original team formed the core of the execution team, so that Big Data could get in place faster.

Your Next Actions

- ☐ Sketch out the key teams and functions that need to be engaged in order to take an innovation from idea to launch, by phase of the idea. In your current state, how cross-functional are the early stages? How could you engage with other groups sooner?

- ☐ Copy the matrix from Figure 5.3, write in a few of your own teams and functions, and shade in the rows or columns that represent reporting relationships. Reflect on the flow of knowledge and resources from programs to functions and back.

- ☐ If you lead or sponsor innovation programs, review the role definitions in this chapter and look for any gaps in your personal skills. Then find one way to close one of these gaps and take action on it.

CHAPTER SIX

Rapid Learning Cycles

In March 2016, four people from Trimax Mowers attended a Rapid Learning Cycles workshop with me in Hamilton, New Zealand. One of them, Jason Low, had just been hired to head Design and Innovation for the company that makes large commercial mowers used to maintain golf courses and harvest hay.

Their office is in the Bay of Plenty, about ninety minutes' drive from Hamilton. By the time they arrived home after the workshop, they decided to reset all of their innovation programs with Rapid Learning Cycles. Jason said, "It just made so much sense."

The Rapid Learning Cycles framework is the heart of High Velocity Innovation and the place at which most companies start. The Rapid Learning Cycles framework eliminates many of the long, slow loopbacks that characterize most innovation programs. Figure 6.1 on page 90 shows the experience that teams have on a typical program without Rapid Learning Cycles.

This was a message that resonated with the team from Trimax because their company prides itself on the longevity of its products, which have to be maintained and supported in the field. This small, family-owned company can't afford the risk that one of their mowers will require a recall to fix a problem, and the seasonality of the market means they also need to deliver new products when their customers have the budget to invest in new equipment.

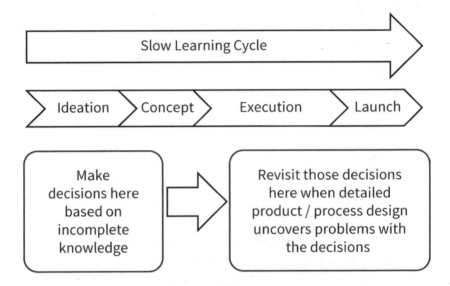

Figure 6.1: Most innovation programs are one long slow loopback.

The framework proved its worth when Jason's team discovered a structural issue in a CAD model that would not have surfaced until they invested in a prototype. During the next two and a half years, Rapid Learning Cycles became central to the innovation system at Trimax. Michael Sievwright, the CEO said, "We have to be smart to succeed globally from New Zealand. For us, innovation drives the value that allows us to compete."

Rapid Learning Cycles Pulls Strong Innovation Practices

The Rapid Learning Cycles framework supports innovation by encouraging teams to learn earlier, before they need to make the decisions that could trigger long, slow loopbacks late in development. Figure 6.2 shows

how Rapid Learning Cycles break innovation work down into short, fast
cycles of experimentation.

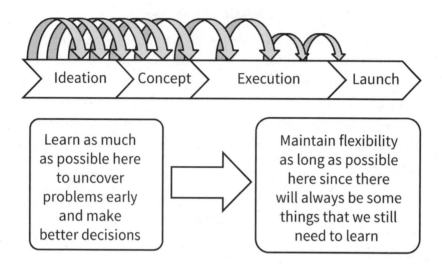

Figure 6.2: Rapid Learning Cycles accelerates innovation by breaking up
long, slow learning cycles.

If you have the ideal team structure and a good strategy, Rapid
Learning Cycles will help accomplish your strategic objectives when you
need them to be done, by avoiding long, slow loopbacks.

If you don't, then Rapid Learning Cycles is the place to start because
it will pull stronger strategies, better team structures, and the other elements of the framework. The practices within Rapid Learning Cycles are
elements that a team can experiment with on their own. When the team
is ready, they can move into a full pilot of the method, and then into the
full High Velocity Innovation system.

The implementation details of the Rapid Learning Cycles framework are beyond the scope of this book; my second book, *The Shortest Distance Between You and Your New Product,* reviews the details of
the framework that an implementation team needs to know. Here, I'll

explain why innovation teams need to run their programs differently, define the elements of the framework, and share how these pieces fit together to accelerate innovation.

Rapid Learning Cycles Adapts Agile

In Chapter Three, I mentioned that Agile Software Development practices didn't translate well for physical products. The teams developing these products have challenges that the developers of Agile didn't need to worry about, like setting up a production line or purchasing tools. Agile practices assume low cost-of-change, few dependencies between user stories (features), and developers who can readily take on any task.

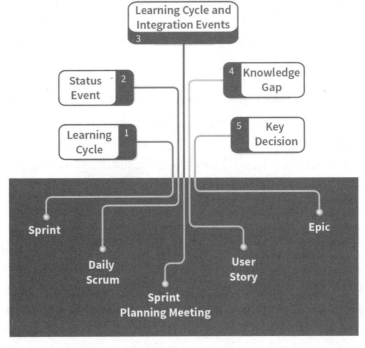

Figure 6.3: The Agile roots of the Rapid Learning Cycles framework.

The Rapid Learning Cycles framework adapts some elements of Agile for an environment of high uncertainty and high cost-of-change, alongside other realities of tangible product development. In this environment, the way to build velocity is to make decisions at the right time with higher confidence so that those decisions won't have to be revisited later. Figure 6.3 on page 92 shows the Agile roots of the Rapid Learning Cycles framework.

When a team can do that, they can move smoothly from Exploration to Investigation to Execution without looping back because a major decision didn't work out as expected. They've eliminated the obstacles that slow down innovation programs or cause them to deliver disappointing results. They've solved the problems that a product team has when they build a physical product.

If you're familiar with Scrum, then you'll see in Figure 6.3 that I adapted the elements in the Scrum framework in specific ways. The use of new terms is intentional; a lot of the teams I work with use Scrum for their software teams, and a few have even tried to use Scrum for physical products. I found that it's much less confusing for everyone when Rapid Learning Cycles uses different terms, because the nature of the work that we are describing is much different than the work being done on a software program using Scrum.

The Nature of Work for a Physical Product

The key insight that drove the development of the Rapid Learning Cycles framework is that the nature of the work in software is different than the nature of the work in a program to develop a physical product.

Software code, hardware designs, and chemical formulations all contain the development team's knowledge; the difference is, the best way to build that knowledge in software is to build the software and test it. The unit of work is the completed software that has been built, tested, and integrated successfully into the full product.

Aside from throwaway prototypes and test harnesses, software teams mainly produce things that end up directly in the final product as compiled code. When it's finished, so is the product, or at least that piece of it. As I described in Chapter Three, it costs little aside from the development and testing effort itself to release a new version of the software, and that software will be an exact replica.

For Software Teams, the Unit of Work Is a User Story

Software teams that use the most common variants of Agile break down features into user stories: short descriptions of a user's interaction with the app. The user can be a person, a device, or another service, and the purpose of a user story is to do something meaningful with the app, which can be as simple as logging in or as complex as launching a spaceship. Some methods classify large user stories as Epics and then break them down into smaller user stories: validate the launch order, perform system Go/No-Go checks, notify the astronauts and grounds crew, and so on.

Once a user story is done, so is the code. If it's for an app, it's ready to upload to the app store or push out to a cloud server. If it's embedded software, it's ready to be loaded onto the chip. The two things that constrain software release timing are the time it takes to run regression tests to make sure the new code didn't break anything else, and the ability of the user community to tolerate the update, as constant updates are annoying.

Two other aspects of software development are assumed to be present on an Agile team: these user stories, even the ones associated with Epics, are self-contained and not dependent on other user stories, especially once the first few development cycles have built the necessary infrastructure. This means that they can be done in any order. The prioritization is driven by customer need and business value.

Then any person on the team can handle any user story, at least in a pinch. If the UI developer gets overloaded, the others can pitch in. They may not be as efficient, but they can get the job done.

Agile Software Development practices like user stories, Demos, Daily Builds, and Test-Driven Development are built on the assumption that the unit of work can be encapsulated in working code, which is completed during a single development cycle. A lot of effort goes into breaking up the large user stories into smaller pieces that fit this criterion. That effort improves software teams' productivity by breaking up large batches of work so that problems come to the surface faster and work flows better through the whole process.

Agile for Tangible Products Is Not as Helpful

In the physical world, it's not so easy to break features down into user stories that are independent of each other. Even a basic feature like turning on the ignition in a car requires most of the car to exist. Until it is, the best an engineer can do is mock-up the experience to learn how it should work. It will have to be finalized when enough of the pieces come together, and they don't come together all at once.

It's possible to use Agile software methods for managing the activities of engineering and other aspects of innovation. An Engineering team that makes a new cell phone, SUV, or laundry detergent builds the product "pattern" in the form of engineering drawings and CAD models, process definitions for assembly, supply chains, and formulations. Some teams have put these deliverables into user stories, alongside other work such as customer visits, usability studies, and pre-promotion work.

But that doesn't help them as much as it helps the Software teams because the problem isn't the prioritization of a list of things that could be done; it's the flow of knowledge to support decisions about many things that must be done.

The Flow of Knowledge Into Design Decisions

These deliverables capture the team's design decisions that get embedded into vendor and reseller commitments, physical tools like molds for plastic parts, and ultimately into an assembly line. Unlike software code, these things can't be easily changed. Unlike most user stories, they need to be done in a specific order with dependencies between these activities. And unlike on a Software team, there are more team members with specialized expertise that is not interchangeable.

For hardware and other physical products, builds cost too much and take too long to serve as the primary way that the team learns. They have to find other ways to build knowledge about the product that help them learn faster and with fewer resources. To go fast, they need to learn as much as they can through modeling, simulations, and subsystem prototypes before undertaking an expensive, lengthy full prototype.

For teams building physical products, the unit of work is the experiment. An experiment is finished when it proves or disproves a hypothesis about an aspect of the product. We call this "closing a Knowledge Gap," and we call the development cycle a "learning cycle."

This is why Epics become Key Decisions. They are the high-impact/high-unknown decisions that drive product success or failure. User stories become Knowledge Gaps, the main unit of work. To find the Key Decisions and Knowledge Gaps, we look for the NUDs parts of the program.

Sprint Planning Events become Learning Cycle and Integration Events that focus on sharing knowledge and making decisions. We use different words because the nature of the work is different: it's focused on learning and decision making instead of building code.

Pull Learning Forward—Push Decisions Later

It takes time to build up the knowledge a team needs to make its most important decisions. The program's NUDs don't just highlight the Knowledge Gaps. They also point to the areas in which the team's instincts are the most likely to lead them astray. The Knowledge Gaps expose the "known unknowns," but NUDs also have "unknown unknowns."

Figure 6.4 shows that the Rapid Learning Cycles framework encourages teams to pull learning forward, in other words, to close Knowledge Gaps early. It also encourages them to push decisions later, all the way to the "last responsible moment" for making a decision. This is difficult to do in most companies, especially in the United States, where Americans have a bias toward acting quickly and decisively. But it is the secret to faster innovation because it keeps teams from making the kinds of missteps that only slow them down right when they can least afford it.

I first encountered the idea of the "last responsible moment" from Mary Poppendieck, whose work explored the connections between Agile Software Development and Lean Manufacturing.[1] The last responsible moment is the last point in time you can make a decision before you start to impact the people downstream of you. Decisions made before this point can still be changed without making anyone too upset or bothered. Decisions made after this point in time can be prohibitively expensive and put the launch schedule at risk.

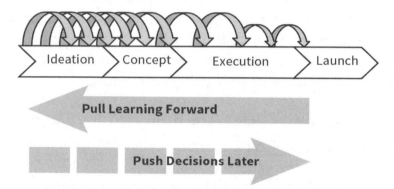

Figure 6.4: Teams running Rapid Learning Cycles pull learning forward and push decisions later.

Normally this also means that the cost-of-change goes up, sometimes dramatically. Suppliers begin charging expediting fees or air freight. Time for critical certification tests get squeezed. Key documents go under regulatory control, meaning that changes require a much more extensive change-control process. Tools need to be rebuilt if they can't be easily fixed.

For as long as I have been working with innovation teams, I encourage them to think more about the last responsible moment, and I know it's difficult to do. Yet in my experience, major decisions that get made too early often get revisited, sometimes later than the last responsible moment.

This isn't anybody's fault; the team just didn't have the knowledge it needed when the sponsors made the decision. Sometimes these decisions get revisited because new information came to light, and sometimes they get revisited because they are the only places where things can still flex to fix problems in other areas.

Yet when a major decision gets made, other decisions and deliverables get built around it, and all that work has to be redone, which adds cost and time to the program. When a team holds these decisions open, that work gets set aside while the team focuses on the more certain parts of the system. When the team finalizes the decision, the other things around it can be finalized, and all of it is much less likely to shift.

Of course, delaying a decision also gives the team more time to learn about the decision so that it can be made using the best available information at the time. The learning inside Rapid Learning Cycles is focused on making these decisions with greater confidence.

Rapid Learning Cycles Are Built Around Learning

The central element of Rapid Learning Cycles, the heart of the heart of High Velocity Innovation, is the learning cycle. This short, focused period of work seeks to answer the team's questions regarding an aspect of their program so that they can make better decisions. During a learning cycle, team members build knowledge about these questions, and then at the end of a learning cycle, they share what they learned with their teams then decide what to learn next.

Like Agile's Sprints, these learning cycles work best when they are on a regular cadence: every two, three, or four weeks. That helps the team stay coordinated. They end with an event at which team members get to show their work, and then re-plan their next cycle of work. The team uses a visual planning board to organize their plan, either on whiteboards with sticky notes or in virtual planning tools online. But the work represented by those sticky notes is completely different than it is with Agile.

Because the team's focus is on knowledge building, the team must be aligned around the overall program direction before they start. Each Rapid Learning Cycles program begins with a Kickoff Event to build this alignment. The first task of a Kickoff Event is to define the team's Core Hypothesis.

The Core Hypothesis Defines the Product

The Core Hypothesis is a short description of the product vision that the team develops during one of their first meetings. The team develops it together so that all team members are aligned about the product's most important objectives. It describes the reasons why the team believes this idea will create customer and business value.

In Chapter Three, I shared this example Core Hypothesis from Agersens:

> The eShepherd is a full virtual fencing solution from the collar to the app that eliminates the need for physical fences as it provides better information about the location of each member of a herd to increase production and lower costs so that we grow Agersens into profitability.

You can see that this example includes the technology (virtual fencing) that will deliver customer value (increase production and lower costs) and business value (growth) with enough specificity to give direction without overconstraining the solution.

The Core Hypothesis will point the team toward some of the most important early learning they can do: develop better knowledge about the concept's soundness as a product. The team will either validate the assumptions embedded in the Core Hypothesis or demonstrate that the product concept has some fundamental flaws before the company spends time and money on it.

The Core Hypothesis may change as the team deepens its understanding of the technology, customers, and markets. In fact, if it's a truly new idea, the Core Hypothesis often changes a lot as the team learns more about potential customers and markets. But it should not drift. When it changes, the program team and all the stakeholders need to know why, so that they can get realigned on the program's new direction.

The Core Hypothesis plays such a central role because it provides guidance to the team as they define and make their most important decisions. I coach Innovation Program Managers to make sure that teams develop this statement themselves. This is a great way to surface any misalignments within the team and address them right away. Then I tell them to allow this process to take the time that it takes. Fifteen extra minutes of discussion can save fifteen days of time lost to a misunderstanding between subsystem owners.

Key Decisions Drive Product Success

A Key Decision is a significant decision that has high impact on a product's ultimate success, and that the team does not have the knowledge to make with confidence. Innovation teams handle these decisions carefully because they make or break the program.

An innovation team will make thousands of decisions before the product launches or the process goes live. But not all of those decisions have the same importance. Some are relatively easy to change later. Others affect

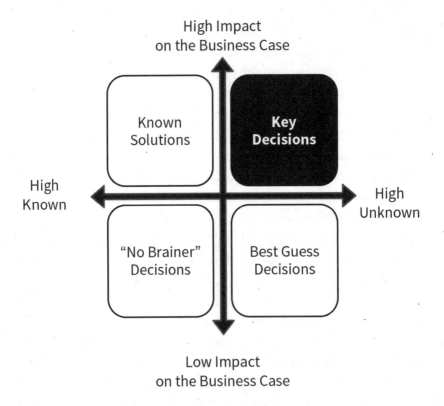

Figure 6.5: Key Decisions are high impact/high unknown decisions.

only a small part of the system. These low-impact decisions don't need special attention because if the team gets one wrong, they can change it easily or it doesn't matter in the end. Key Decisions are the ones the team needs to get right the first time, or the product will go on a long detour.

Figure 6.5 shows how we decide whether or not a decision is a Key Decision. Other decisions leverage known solutions. Many arise naturally out of the team members' experience and the knowledge readily available to them. Some decisions get imposed on the team by technology or market constraints. Key Decisions are the ones that enable the product to do something new, unique, or different than previous products.

You can find your program's Key Decisions by asking, "What's new, unique, or difficult about this program?" These NUDs are, by definition, Key Decisions. They can come from the technical side, the commercial side, or from other places, like Legal or Regulatory Affairs. Additional Key Decisions are identified when you look for other decisions that rise to the same level as your NUDs in terms of impact on the program and lack of knowledge needed to make the decision.

Key Decisions have a sequence that reflects the process for executing the innovation. When teams understand how Key Decisions flow into one another, the sequence and timing for these decisions, and who is responsible for making decisions, they will be prepared to make these decisions with confidence at the right time. They will be much less likely to be revisited, and that will help the entire program run at higher velocity.

Knowledge Gaps Highlight Learning to Be Done

A Knowledge Gap is something the decision maker needs to know in order to make a Key Decision with confidence. In the Rapid Learning Cycles framework, the Knowledge Gap is the unit of work that gets managed: they get assigned to owners, prioritized, and tracked as they close. Knowledge Gap owners produce short reports to capture what they learned to close a Knowledge Gap, and this gets incorporated into the related Key Decision recommendation.

Innovation teams always have more Knowledge Gaps than they can close. Much of the "art" of leading a Rapid Learning Cycles program is learning to prioritize: which Knowledge Gaps to close early, which ones to defer, and which ones to consciously leave open so that the team can make its most important decisions with the best available knowledge.

By definition, every Key Decision has at least one Knowledge Gap to close before the decision can be made. When the team creates the first-pass list of Knowledge Gaps, they turn to their map of Key Decisions to identify the Knowledge Gaps related to those decisions. These Knowledge Gaps drive the team's work during the early phases, and help the team continue to eliminate risk and integrate new information in later phases.

Deliverables Encapsulate Decisions

Deliverables are the final products of an innovation and include the product or new process. In the early phases, the deliverable can be as simple as a concept proposal that fleshes out the idea enough to be compared with others. In mid-development, deliverables include things like Proof-of-Concepts, draft execution plans and budgets, and business case analyses. The final phases are primarily about producing the deliverables that bring the idea to life: manufacturing tools, marketing collateral, and changes to process documentation.

Both traditional and Agile program management focus on completing deliverables: requirements, documents, and other tasks for traditional program management and user stories for Agile. With Rapid Learning Cycles, the deliverable is the way that an innovation team communicates its decisions to partners. Instead of focusing on producing these deliverables, the focus is on understanding the Key Decision sequence and then managing the work to close Knowledge Gaps so that the deliverables get produced on time.

Learning Cycle Teams and Closing Knowledge Gaps

In Chapter Three, I introduced the Design–Experiment–Capture method of learning. This is what happens inside a learning cycle. Someone on your team who owns a Knowledge Gap will:

- Design a way to close that Knowledge Gap with an experiment or other learning activity.

- Run the experiment or do the activity.
- Capture what has been learned.

The cycle isn't done until all three of those steps have been finalized. I coach team members to start working on their Knowledge Gaps by doing a first-pass experimental design and then sharing that with their peers to get feedback on it.

They will close out a learning cycle by writing a Knowledge Gap Report, a short summary of what they did, what they learned, and what they recommend as next steps. That report captures the knowledge they built for their current team and for future teams who may encounter similar gaps. They will share that report at their Learning Cycle Event.

Events Pull Real-Time Knowledge Capture

At the end of every learning cycle, teams have Learning Cycle Events to share what they learned. When it's time to make Key Decisions, teams have Integration Events to bring together the decision makers and the knowledge the team has built to close the decisions. Both events pull the work of innovation by building urgency and accountability into the process as they drive real-time knowledge capture. Figure 6.6 shows how this works within a phase of development.

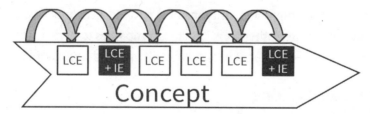

Figure 6.6: Each learning cycle concludes with a Pull Event.

Knowledge work tends to expand to fill the available time, so innovation teams place a strict limit on that time before requiring teams to share what they have learned. Every learning cycle is a timebox: a fixed amount of time that the team will use to learn as much as it can about its Knowledge Gaps. Within that time, team members can structure their work in any way that maximizes learning.

Integration Events not only serve as the focus for getting clear decisions, they also keep Innovation Sponsors engaged and informed about the true state of the programs they sponsor. The Innovation Sponsors and other stakeholders get a chance to see the team learning in real-time, provide feedback on the team's Key Decisions and Knowledge Gaps, and review the results of their experimentation.

Rapid Learning Cycles Pull Better Decisions

A key benefit for Trimax has been the way that Rapid Learning Cycles drives the team to ask, "What do we already know, and what knowledge do we need to make this decision?" The group has a lot of collective knowledge about how to build mowers; now more of that knowledge is captured in a way that makes it easier to make decisions. Jason said, "The process has helped us think more deeply about our decisions. Before going into an Integration Event, we ask ourselves, 'Is it really the right time for us to make this decision? Are we at that last responsible moment?'"

In the summer of 2018, Jason's team kicked off a new program for a wider mower with more features. After more than two years of running programs with Rapid Learning Cycles they had a knowledge library to build upon. That helped reduce the number of NUDs for this program so that they can accelerate development even more. Meanwhile, Trimax has become one of the biggest champions of the Rapid Learning Cycles framework. They encourage other New Zealand companies to increase their global competitiveness by using it to accelerate the pace of innovation.

Your Next Actions

- ☐ Identify some examples of long, slow loopbacks you have experienced in your own programs. How could early learning have prevented them?

- ☐ Identify a few Key Decisions for your current program, then break them down into the Knowledge Gaps you need to close to make the decision with greater confidence.

- ☐ Make a plan to close one of those Knowledge Gaps, and a two-week deadline to close it. Then execute that plan over the next two weeks.

CHAPTER SEVEN

INNOVATION PROGRAM MANAGEMENT

Celia Cheng is the head of the Program Management Office for SunPower, a solar energy company based in Silicon Valley. Five years ago, she and the team were exploring ways to improve their development process. That's when they encountered Rapid Learning Cycles, and she began coaching her teams on the RLC framework.

She started guiding her Program Managers on using RLC concepts as part of their regular thought process in managing programs, to drive decision making, using it where and when it made sense.

At the 2017 Rapid Learning Cycles Virtual Summit, Celia said, "Our product development really varies from solar cell technology to modules to complete solutions in different spaces. One size doesn't fit all. . . . You have to know what problem you're trying to solve and you really have to think about the intent."

If a Program Manager on Celia's team tries to run the early phases of an Innovation Program using the same toolset that he or she uses to execute a standard product development program, the tools will start to break down under the stress of constant change. Yet if the Program Manager continues to bring the investigation toolset into the later phases, those tools will break down, too. A Program Manager responsible for driving innovation from idea to launch needs a diverse toolset and the discernment to know when to switch from one tool to another as the program moves from ideation through concept to execution.

Celia said, "I coach my Program Managers to focus on making the right decisions. What are the decisions we need to make? When do we need to make them? And then as far as Learning Cycle Events, I leave that to the R&D Engineering Team and Business Leads to work out these details."

Innovation Program Leaders coach their teams on how and when to use the tools of Project Management. In fact, it's better if the team learns these tools together, and then collectively decides how to use them for the phase of the program that they are in. This strategy builds alignment around working methods that allow the team to focus on the work in front of them for their program's specific phase and next major milestone.

Innovation Programs Experience More Change and Risk

Innovation programs need specific tools because they experience more change and risk than other programs. An incremental product release, a new production facility, or a small change to improve customer service has more known than unknown about how to do it. Innovation programs usually have much more that is unknown, and the innovation team has to constantly integrate new information as it comes in. Yet the decisions they make here have long-term implications for the success of the idea, and therefore the entire Innovation Program.

Innovation programs vary widely on the amount of risk that's acceptable before moving into execution, the cost of making a decision that needs to be revisited, and the amount of uncertainty that exists from what the team needs to learn. Figure 7.1 shows that different types of programs need different toolsets, depending on the degree of uncertainty and cost-of-change.

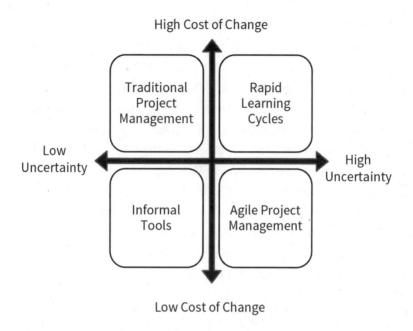

Figure 7.1: Project Management methods application matrix.

Informal Tools

Programs with low uncertainty and low cost-of-change hardly need managing at all; a simple action list will be sufficient. The team can predict what needs to go on the action list; if they're wrong, they can just change it. Only the smallest of innovations go in this quadrant.

For Innovation Programs, I typically see engineers using such informal tools to manage their own work to close Knowledge Gaps or produce deliverables. I encourage that rather than forcing the Program Manager to track levels of detail that aren't useful for the team or its stakeholders. The well-functioning Engineering Team doesn't have time for micromanagement at this level.

Traditional Project Management Tools

Programs with high cost-of-change and low uncertainty work best with traditional project management tools and strong change control. These are the methods that most people learn in Project Management 101 courses: Gantt charts and PERT charts, critical path analysis, issues logs, buffers, and schedule optimization. They originally came out of the first modern large-scale construction projects in the late 1800s and efforts to plan troop movements during World War I.

For a team that needs to build a production line or distribution network, these tools play a valuable role once the Key Decisions are mostly closed. By this point in development, the cost-of-change remains high and gets higher by the day. But the uncertainty has been reduced, so the program team isn't hit by constant change. The teams shift from learning to doing and need to stay coordinated. These methods excel at tracking dependencies and optimizing the best way to get to the final goal, once that goal is known in sufficient detail.

A lot of authors from the Agile community equate these tools with waterfall development, which means teams must have all the requirements done before commencing any system architecture work. Then that has to be done before any implementation work. The same rigid boundaries proceed to the end.

We've known for decades now that waterfall development doesn't work well for anything that hasn't been done before. The more NUDs a program has, the more likely it is to experience a catastrophic failure when forced into a waterfall model from the beginning. The team is forced to make decisions with very little knowledge about the final result. This triggers massive loopbacks.

Waterfall programs use traditional tools. That has led some people to abandon these methods in all cases, even when the program to be managed has a lot of dependencies and low uncertainties. Waterfall-based programs have problems because waterfall doesn't work; the traditional tools work well when freed from the constraints of a waterfall process.

Agile Project Management Tools

Agile Software Development methods are tailored for the fast pace of consumer software, smartphone app, and Software-as-a-Service (SaaS) development. In this world, cost-of-change is very low because changes can be pushed out to customers as soon as they are tested.

This is the best method for the Execution Phases of programs that can be changed easily and at low risk. As I described in Chapter Three, it's not the best method for early development, especially if the innovation team makes decisions that will be costly to revisit later.

Rapid Learning Cycles

This method is tailored for the early phases of innovations that have both high uncertainty and high cost-of-change. Like Agile, it helps teams manage uncertainty and integrate new information as it comes in by planning and working in short bursts. But unlike Agile, it recognizes the need to make decisions at the right time and by the right people so that these decisions don't have to be revisited later.

Rapid Learning Cycles also reinforces a shift from doing to learning in early development when learning is much more important. In these learning phases, a team doesn't build a CAD model because it's on the project plan. The team builds the CAD model because it's the best way to learn specific things that will help them close Knowledge Gaps.

Right Tools for the Phase and Nature of the Work

I work a lot with consumer electronics. In that world, we may have Agile, traditional Project Management, and Rapid Learning Cycles on the same program. The Software and firmware teams run Agile the whole time, the hardware development teams run traditional program management during late development, and all of the teams use Rapid Learning Cycles to close Knowledge Gaps and make Key Decisions with greater confidence.

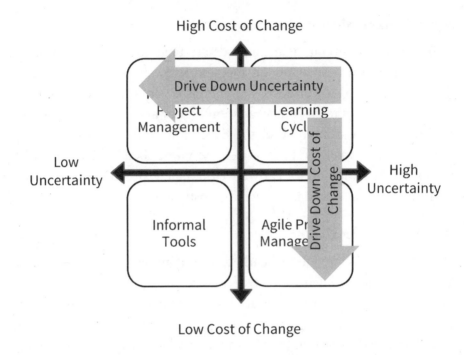

Figure 7.2: Rapid Learning Cycles strengthen the other methods.

Figure 7.2 shows that Rapid Learning Cycles strengthen the other methods. For programs with high cost-of-change (anything that requires production and distribution) Rapid Learning Cycles help eliminate uncertainty. As decisions get finalized, the Program Manager can use traditional program management for the execution of those decisions to ensure that everything gets done in the right sequence to optimize the schedule.

But even Agile teams can benefit from targeted Rapid Learning Cycles. These teams make early architecture, technology partner, and market fit decisions that are difficult to undo later. For these teams, Rapid Learning Cycles helps them make decisions that increase their flexibility. For the product, solid architecture, dependable partners, and a deep understanding of the market make it easier for developers to use Agile to build the system because good decisions lower the cost-of-change.

Flexible Phase Gate Processes Support Innovation

I said in Chapter Three that phase gate product development programs have become ubiquitous for managing innovation; some groups even manage business process and operational innovations with some form of it. If your company is past the startup phase and doesn't have a phase gate process, this is another relatively quick win: start with the basic model shown in Figure 7.3 and then iterate and adjust until it fits. You'll know it's working if a team can celebrate an early failure.

Phase Gate Product Development Process

Figure 7.3: A phase gate process for innovation.

Phase gate processes support innovation by providing clear points for the business to determine whether or not to continue investing in developing an innovation. Figure 7.3 shows a simple phase gate process for innovation programs. The dark arrows in between the phases represent those business control points, or gates.

Strict Waterfall Phase Gates Slow Down Innovation

When this type of process was introduced, organizations tended to define these gates strictly, so that teams had to pass through a gate before being allowed to start any of the downstream phases work. This reinforces a strict waterfall process, even more so because people often labeled their phases like this:

Requirements > Architecture / System Design >
Detailed Design > Verification and Validation > Launch

That's a waterfall process embedded and enforced via phase gates, and products put through this process are likely to get stuck in the later phases because teams are forced to revisit decision after decision from earlier phases. But that's not a characteristic inherent in phase gate processes.

The other problem with such rigid phase gates is that every gate accumulates checklist items and deliverables from groups as wide-ranging as Brand Standards, Regulatory Affairs, Legal, Finance, and Procurement. I've had to help many teams identify what deliverables were truly valuable and what was just a distraction. All of these documents turn the weeks prior to a gate into a massive paperwork exercise to check all the boxes, instead of a time to prep the leadership team for the investment decision they are about to make.

Completing all of this work tends to encourage people to get more attached to passing the gate, because the preliminary work is already done. I've been to Gate Reviews during which presenting such deliverables was the primary thing on the agenda, and the team assumed they would either pass or be given a chance to correct any issues. The business decision that was the original purpose for the gate had faded into the background.

Drive Gate Decisions Around Business Control Points

It's far better for the leadership team to ask where and how they want to make investment decisions for innovation programs. The simple model in Figure 7.3 gives them four control points:

1. Whether or not to invest a small amount of money and a small team to develop a Proof-of-Concept.

2. Whether or not to carry that investment forward to build a feasible product design for production.

3. Whether or not to invest in the production tooling and components needed to support launch.

4. Whether or not to commit to launch with distributors and channel partners.

Those control points come with increased expectations for the team's ability to hit the targets set for the product and increased confidence in the business value of the product for the business. For example, a team may have a target market window for Gate 1 that they can adjust at Gate 2, with a target launch date. By Gate 3 they should be ready to commit to an actual launch date, and at Gate 4, they confirm that they will hit it. They'll converge in a similar way on cost targets, forecasted unit volumes, feature sets, and quality goals.

Ideally, a product can be stopped at any control point. In practice, once programs have made it through Gate 2, they're only stopped if a major problem emerges that gets the team stuck for too long without making progress. For dysfunctional innovation systems, momentum carries a team through. For healthy ones, the risks have been mostly eliminated by Gate 2.

Flexible Phase Gates Work Best

In practice, phase gate models work better when they stay focused on these business decisions but retain flexibility, especially concerning factors such as when to begin working with suppliers and when to order tooling and components that have long lead times. You can get your products to market faster if you engage with suppliers early, because then their best available knowledge gets embedded in the product design. In the long run, it will be much less expensive than holding back information about the program. You just need to make sure that ideas and possibilities are not misinterpreted as decisions.

There is no reason to delay a program by weeks or months to meet an arbitrary business rule about when to spend money on tools. Spending some early money on long lead time parts and tools can save a lot of development time and effort. The team runs some risk that these early commitments will need to be changed, but if they focused on making their Key Decisions at the right time with the right knowledge, that risk will be lowered.

With a flexible phase gate process, designs freeze the way a pond does, instead of the way that a flash-frozen raspberry does. As the design starts to freeze, teams start to work downstream on the parts that are solid, while other elements are still floating. The team accepts a small risk that the frozen parts will thaw, but they can lower that risk with Rapid Learning Cycles. Even if they do rework a few things, they'll still be faster and less costly overall than if they had waited to start anything until everything was frozen.

The Three Stages of an Innovation Program

Whereas some innovations are small enough to be put in place immediately, and others are so compelling that they skip some early phases, most innovation programs go through three major stages of development that loosely correspond to the phases in a phase gate lifecycle. Whether you break up these stages into multiple phases or keep them in one phase, and whether a program moves fast or slow, this is the default pattern for innovation.

The Exploration Stage (Pre-Concept)

Many companies suffer from too many good ideas, and others claim that they don't have enough. The Exploration Phase is a time to gather the ideas for an innovation into one space where they can be compared. The company may seek a new business model to prevent disruption by others, develop new lines of business to drive organic growth, or achieve a breakthrough in operational efficiency and cost structures.

The Innovation Program Leader's role in the Exploration Phase is to facilitate the team and the organization through the process of finding new ideas (ideation) and perform some first-pass screening on those ideas to get them down to a few for further investigation. This is the time when tools that encourage creative thinking and build customer empathy are especially important because they help a team move beyond the company's present into its future.

The program works best with an adaptation of Rapid Learning Cycles to ensure that teams stay focused on developing innovations to answer the company's specific strategic needs. The main difference is that teams will track their ideas as Key Decisions like this: "Will we invest time and resources into the next phase of development for this idea?"

The Knowledge Gaps become the questions the team needs to answer in order to make a recommendation to their leadership team about the idea. They may have questions about markets, customers, competitors, business model alternatives, or advanced research results.

They'll probably need to interview potential customers and distributors, pull and analyze market data, build some first-pass financial models, and get some quick input on technical feasibility. They may need to build a quick-and-dirty prototype to validate whether or not to invest in something more. By the end of this stage, they should have a good idea about the major NUDs that the team will need to solve in the next phase.

The Exploration Phase concludes with the decision to build an Investigation Team that will develop the idea into a concept that the company can execute—or the decision not to pursue the idea. It's better to choose a handful of ideas and then eliminate the rest.

The Investigation Stage (Concept and Design)

This is the time to focus attention on a specific idea to develop it into a concept. The team will develop a Core Hypothesis that they'll test in this phase: the technical, customer, and business dimensions of the idea under investigation. Along the way, they may build a Proof–of–Concept, run a small pilot, and try out different implementation approaches.

The Innovation Program Leader's role in this stage is to help the team characterize the value of the idea, identify major questions to answer about this idea before it can move into execution, understand the risks they'll need to eliminate or mitigate in the Execution Phase, and build support for the idea among company stakeholders. The tools here help the Program Manager and the team learn about the idea as fast as possible and adapt their plans as new information comes in about the idea.

Rapid Learning Cycles is tailored for this phase of innovation. I started to see some groups pair this with a lightweight traditional project plan because the number of deliverables for this phase begins to increase. This is also when the Software teams will start to run Agile for a program, although they too should be encouraged to identify their NUDs and use them to identify Key Decisions that have high cost-of-change.

Figure 7.4 shows how the Learning Cycles Plan defines the work to be done in this phase. Teams define their Learning Plans one phase at a time and aim their Key Decisions and Knowledge Gaps toward answering the questions they need to pass through the next gate.

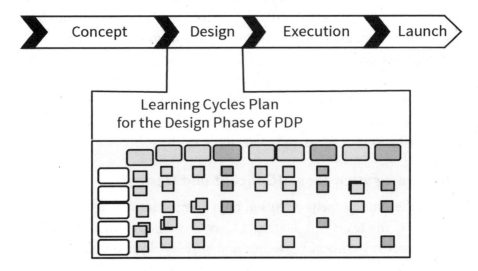

Figure 7.4: Rapid Learning Cycles within a phase.

By the end of the Investigation Stage, the idea has become a concept with a business case. This phase ends with a clear decision to take this idea into Execution—or not, if the business case isn't strong enough.

The Execution Stage (Execution and Launch)

In this phase, the concept gets realized: the product gets put into mass production, the new business model gets launched, and the new organizational structures, IT tools, or cost-saving measures get put into place. The team will spend most of their time here executing decisions they made in the last stage.

The Innovation Program Leader's role here is to manage the uncertainties that remain in the program as it moves through execution. Unlike programs with more certainty, innovation programs still have the need to integrate new information, adjust to plans that don't work as expected, and manage the company's expectations about early results.

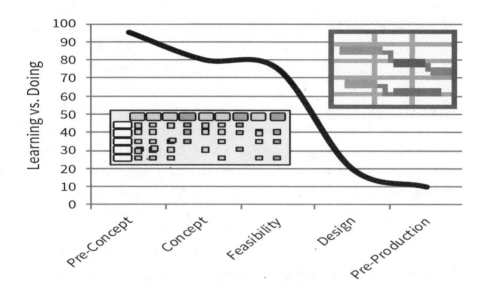

Figure 7.5: The transition from Learning to Execution.

Figure 7.5 shows how Project Management tools shift as the innovation moves toward maturity. Depending on the type of innovation, the Program Manager may use traditional tools such as Gantt charts and change control, Agile tools such as Scrum or Scaled Agile Framework (SAFe), or a hybrid of both. Meanwhile, the team may continue to spin Rapid Learning Cycles on areas of outstanding risk.

Even as the team moves toward traditional tools, by now they will have a strong sense of cadence and the value of working in defined cycles that end with an event. Some teams continue to retain this structure, defining the work to be done in the next cycle, then pausing to share their work and make adjustments before deciding what needs to be done in the next cycle. The difference is that teams don't lose sight of all the things that need to be done before launch, the order in which they need to be done, and the impact of changes to the plan this late in development.

A Flexible Approach Focuses Innovation Teams

At SunPower, they introduced phase gates about ten years ago. Their major gate is Gate 2, and they use Rapid Learning Cycles ahead of Gate 2 to get to a Plan of Record. The framework helps them focus on what they need to learn and the decisions they need to make on the front end to get to that point.

Celia's team redesigned their gate approval templates to embed language around Key Decisions and refocus the information that was being presented. This supported the gates so that the decision making aspects of the gates come to the forefront of the meeting, where they should be. The language of Rapid Learning Cycles has helped sponsors understand when they need to give their approval to the Key Decisions and prepare for the gate approvals

Decision makers have a better understanding of what decision they're being asked to make, and also why some decisions are not yet at the last responsible moment. Celia said, "It has changed these reviews into a much more useful kind of discussion."

Your Next Actions

- ☐ Use the matrix in Figure 7.1 to organize the types of work that need to be done for your innovation programs by cost-of-change and uncertainty: hardware development, process development, Procurement, validation & verification, software development, apps, services, and others. Do teams have the flexibility to use the right tools for their work?

- ☐ Make a list of programs that failed to get to launch. When were they cancelled? How could those programs have failed faster?

- ☐ Review your phase gate deliverables checklists. Can you eliminate anything right now?

CHAPTER EIGHT

PLATFORMS AND EXTENSIBLE KNOWLEDGE

In 2014, Sonion embarked on a journey to accelerate the pace of innovation. Sonion makes tiny microphones, speakers, and other components for hearing health and professional audio. The company's product development cycles are tied to their customers' development cycles and most products are built to spec for a specific customer. For a company like this, the ability to leverage knowledge across customers is the key to High Velocity Innovation.

At Sonion, pull for a new innovation system began with a commitment from Freek Blom, the vice president of Research and Development, to "learn as fast as possible." He encouraged his teams to build fast, reusable knowledge throughout their development programs, and he established a "Lean R&D" system that enabled them to maximize value by eliminating the wastes of reinvention, budget overruns, and Manufacturing Startup issues.

In Chapter Three, I shared that the one aspect of Lean Product Development proven to demonstrate results is the set of practices around knowledge flow. Sonion took those recommendations and ran with them.

Innovation teams can't waste time relearning what the organization already knows. Yet people often assume that projects are only innovative if they are completely new—new to the company, new to the world. They tell their teams, "Forget everything you know" and "Start with a blank sheet of paper." As if they could.

All along, we've assumed that you want to achieve High Velocity Innovation without compromising your ability to deliver breakthroughs and even disruptive innovation. When you understand how to deploy extensible knowledge and platforms, even disruptive innovations require less invention. This means that your teams don't need to start with a blank sheet of paper; instead, they figure out what the team already knows and use that as a place to start even if the final destination is far outside the company's normal boundaries.

Innovation Development Is Knowledge Development

When teams first begin using Rapid Learning Cycles, they see that their current program goes faster because they are not experiencing as many long, slow loopbacks. But the real results show up on the next programs, because those teams are able to benefit from the knowledge captured from earlier programs.

As teams start to use the Rapid Learning Cycles framework, they quickly learn the value of knowledge reuse. When they can beg, borrow, or steal knowledge from others to close a Knowledge Gap, they free up time to close another Knowledge Gap. Since teams never have time to close all of the Knowledge Gaps they have, they will be driven to look for such opportunities. The end of every learning cycle occurs when teams capture the new knowledge they have built in the Knowledge Gap Reports they'll use to share this knowledge within their teams.

Although each report is short and focused, it doesn't take very long for a team to develop an impressive body of knowledge, already captured in small pieces that are easier for others to digest and reuse. This knowledge is valuable even if the program is stopped. As a team's innovation leads to the development of a new product, a new product family, or a new business, the value of that knowledge goes up exponentially.

Closing Knowledge Gaps accelerates innovation through better decision making. Capturing that knowledge in real time accelerates the current program when decision makers can make better decisions and accelerate future programs by giving these future teams a better place to start. The current team has made their knowledge available to future teams for reuse and extension.

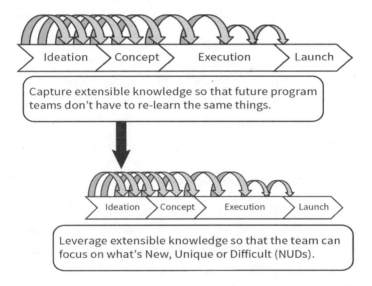

Figure 8.1: Rapid Learning Cycles capture extensible knowledge.

Figure 8.1 shows that future teams can go even faster because their work is grounded in this knowledge. Future teams can focus on their own NUDs rather than reinvention and rework. Some innovation experts claim that this leads only to incremental innovation, which is not very exciting and certainly not disruptive.

The experiences of Sonion and many other companies in this book prove that a library of extensible knowledge is the raw material for innovation. When you understand how your product works at the level of the fundamental science, and you have the same knowledge depth about your customers and markets, then you're in a unique position to identify and solve problems your customers didn't know they had.

For Sonion, the ability to capture its deep knowledge about the science behind its microphones and receivers, and make that knowledge more accessible to its developers, would deliver dividends in faster time-to-market and greater reliability.

In most organizations, however, there is no way to get momentum behind an effort to build such a library of knowledge. Such a project requires strong pull from someplace in the organization, which begins with an appreciation for the value of extensible knowledge and a process that supports real-time knowledge capture as part of the team's core activities, rather than something they do if they have time.

At Sonion, this is one of the key benefits of High Velocity Innovation with Rapid Learning Cycles. They recognize that their teams will never capture extensible knowledge unless knowledge capture is an integrated part of the program.

What Is Extensible Knowledge?

Extensible knowledge is any knowledge that has value outside of the specific problem domain in which it was developed. This includes everything from existing product data and knowledge about current customer behavior to knowledge about your competitors, key suppliers, partners, and the development process. This knowledge can be reused and extended in other domains.

Figure 8.2 shows that the goal of capturing all this knowledge is to turn today's Key Decisions into known solutions on tomorrow's programs so that future product teams can focus on their own NUDs. It's especially helpful for teams to capture the things that didn't work: the options that were explored and abandoned, the experiments that failed, and the pivots the team needed to make.

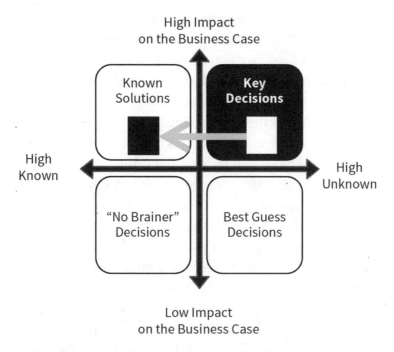

Figure 8.2: Today's Key Decision is tomorrow's known solution.

I call it "extensible" because such knowledge usually gets updated and extended when it gets used, even in a simple incremental product release. When a team is new to High Velocity Innovation, they may lack anything that has the maturity needed for straight reuse. As they start to close Knowledge Gaps and write Knowledge Gap Reports, they'll start to build extensible knowledge quickly.

Extensible Knowledge Is the Raw Material for Innovation

When your teams understand the fundamental physics behind their designs, they have the raw materials to apply that knowledge to new problems that may look nothing like the original problem domain. Basic science includes the social science behind your product: consumer and channel partner behaviors, user interactions, market research data, and field observations. It includes process knowledge, such as the science of efficient validation testing and early integration, as well as product design knowledge about things like materials and components, mechanical stress, electrical interference, and environmental limits.

When people ask innovation teams to start with a blank sheet of paper, what they really mean is that they don't want just an incremental improvement. But the way to get breakthroughs is to start lower down the scale, at the level of the basic science and consumer behavior you want to influence, with knowledge that is built to be extensible.

That allows Sonion, which has a long history in the hearing health area, to extend its reach into professional audio and wearables. The basic science of microphones and receivers doesn't change and the ability to listen to customers who need better solutions for enhancing sound doesn't change. The final product may end up looking completely different to an outsider but the products are built upon a shared base of extensible knowledge.

The A3 Report for Capturing Knowledge

From all my time spent working with Lean Product Development, the A3 Report is the element that has stuck with me the most, and it is what I use most often with my clients. "A3" refers to the paper size that's two A4 (letter) size pages side-by-side. In the United States, the closest equivalent is tabloid or 11 x 17 paper, printed in landscape mode, which is what I use most of the time.

Some authors in the Lean community attempt to overcomplicate the A3 writing process by equating it with problem-solving. For me, the way that this physical form improves communication has applications far beyond the problem-solving A3s from Lean literature. Figures 8.3 and 8.4 show the templates that teams use to capture their Knowledge Gaps and Key Decisions.

This paper size is large enough for a substantial report on one single-sided sheet, but small enough that the entire report is visible within a person's field of vision. The size forces brevity and conciseness that help with clarity. It can be written in an hour or two and read in less than ten minutes. It's easy to view or display on a widescreen monitor or to print in most offices. The amount of text is ideal for capturing one bite-sized piece of knowledge.

PROJECT NAME Knowledge Gap Number		
The Knowledge Gap as a Question **Owner:** **Learning Cycle:**		
The Question to Answer: The Knowledge Gap question **The Purpose** How closing this Knowledge Gap will help the program and why it's important to close. **What We Have Done** A **short** summary of what the team has done in order to close this Knowledge Gap. This can be a summary of the experimental methods or description of other learning activities.	**What We Have Learned** A summary of what the team has learned as they have closed this Knowledge Gap. **Recommendations and Next Steps** What the KG Owner recommends as the next step.	

Figure 8.3: The Knowledge Gap Report.

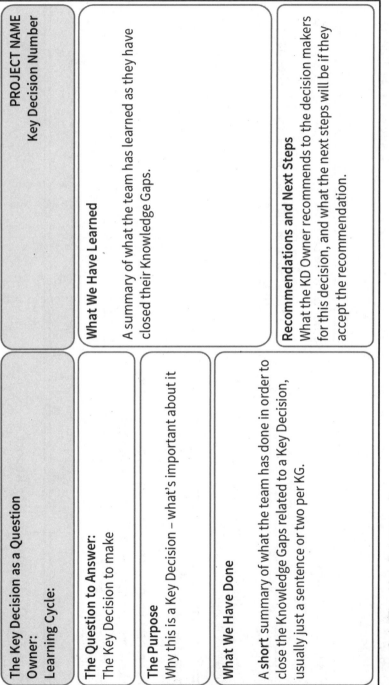

The Key Decision as a Question
Owner:
Learning Cycle:

PROJECT NAME
Key Decision Number

The Question to Answer:
The Key Decision to make

The Purpose
Why this is a Key Decision – what's important about it

What We Have Done

A short summary of what the team has done in order to close the Knowledge Gaps related to a Key Decision, usually just a sentence or two per KG.

What We Have Learned

A summary of what the team has learned as they have closed their Knowledge Gaps.

Recommendations and Next Steps
What the KD Owner recommends to the decision makers for this decision, and what the next steps will be if they accept the recommendation.

Figure 8.4: The Key Decision Report.

Many of the templates on the website are formatted as A3 Reports, including the Key Decision and Knowledge Gap Reports that High Velocity Innovation teams use to capture their knowledge in real time. Sonion learned that it can use the Knowledge Gap template that is part of Rapid Learning Cycles to pull extensible knowledge. The template reinforces good, systematic knowledge creation that leads to understandable, believable, and generalizable knowledge. The recommendations and the results make this knowledge actionable. Their Knowledge Supermarket makes it accessible.

Levels of Extensible Knowledge

The spectrum of extensible knowledge goes from the basic science behind a product all the way to the ecosystems that support Apple's app store and online gamers' mods communities. Figure 8.5 shows that extensible knowledge exists along a spectrum from basic science to a final product's ecosystem. Incremental innovation takes place far to the right, but breakthrough innovation works far to the left.

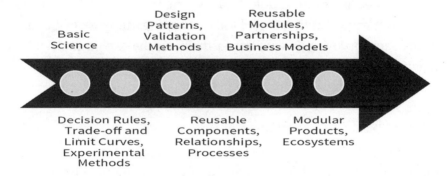

Figure 8.5: Levels of extensible knowledge.

Fundamental Science

The knowledge that a team builds regarding the fundamental science of their work is some of the most highly valued for innovation because those who understand the dynamics of a system are those best prepared to disrupt it. Basic science (and its counterparts in understanding economics, consumer behavior, and design principles) provide the raw materials for innovation by generating possibilities that are not tied to specific implementations.

This is the place to capture knowledge as A3 Reports, like Key Decisions and Knowledge Gaps, that capture one small piece of knowledge independently. More complex ideas, design guides, and handbooks can work, but they take longer to write and are much less likely to be read because of the time investment required. It's better to break such a thing down into a series of A3s that can be populated over time.

Design Patterns

This next level takes fundamental science and applies it to the company's current market needs. If your teams start a new product design by copying the existing design, then they are basically reusing a design pattern. Engineers, formulation chemists, quality engineers, and even advertising groups often start by reusing and extending the work that has been done before.

There is nothing wrong with this type of reuse, but it doesn't lend itself to accelerated innovation. It takes time to remove the elements of the old work product that don't fit before adding in the parts that do fit. Teams can improve this level by formalizing the design patterns into design templates, which give new teams a better place to start. These templates may eventually become platforms.

Platforms

Platforms are bundles of extensible knowledge that are packaged for easy reuse. Software platforms consist of reusable module libraries that use standard interfaces, and teams extend this platform by adding new modules to implement new features. Hardware platforms consist of anything from starter design templates to common parts libraries.

In food and beverage, consumer packaged goods, chemistry, and biology, a "platform" might be a type of formulation that has known parameters and a standard production process, which allows product teams to tweak specific attributes like flavor or cleaning power while keeping the rest of the product essentially the same. In a services industry, the platform might be the starter set of policies, procedures, and methods that needs to be tailored to meet local market or customer needs. The large consulting firms pride themselves on their platforms of proprietary methods that allow junior consultants to quickly address client needs without any prior industry expertise.

A well-documented platform makes incremental innovation much easier because teams know what the platform can accommodate easily, and what will be difficult. They can make better decisions about how to refresh a product for maximum impact with minimal investment. Teams can develop features for the high-end version of a platform, and then release those features to mid- and low-end products as the market matures.

Breakthroughs and disruptive innovations often require new platforms to be developed—but not always. Sometimes, a company can achieve a strategic breakthrough when they find a new customer who can use the same platform with just a little extension to tailor the product. Sometimes, a company can achieve a breakthrough when they use a current platform in a new way that is completely unanticipated by the market.

The size of an innovation isn't tied to the amount of new material in it. The iconic Tesla still relies upon a century of experience developing cars. The iPhone was innovative because it bundled together capabilities that had been evolving for years (touchscreens, cellular antennae, and cellular Internet) into a compelling package.

These innovation teams took existing platforms and recombined them in ways that created compelling new solutions to problems— sometimes problems customers didn't know they had until they saw the product operating.

Ecosystems

When a platform crosses the company boundaries, it becomes an ecosystem. In the virtual world, we recognize these as the iPhone and Android platforms for apps, the Facebook platform for games and social media tools, and the Amazon platform for eCommerce. In these examples, a company developed a standard way to interface with its systems, and then invited others to develop their own uses for those systems. By opening their platforms for other developers, they accelerated the potential for innovation and kept themselves at the center as the arbiter of the platform. They are the ones who have established the standards.

Building and Using Extensible Knowledge

Innovation teams build a lot of knowledge as they move from Concept Evaluation to Proof–of–Concept and Feasibility to execution. The key to building a library of extensible knowledge is the ability to capture it as it is generated, having mechanisms to make that knowledge accessible, and the ability to use that knowledge in a systematic way.

Real-Time Knowledge Capture

Innovation teams build a lot of knowledge quickly; that knowledge will have no value beyond the current product if it is not captured in real time. Rapid Learning Cycles encourage this because team members have to present what they have learned at the end of every learning cycle, in the form of a Knowledge Gap report. Not all Knowledge Gap Reports contain extensible knowledge, but that is not something the team can know in advance or that the organization needs to decide immediately. Knowledge Gap Reports go into a project repository; that is good enough while you still have a handful of programs that are aiming for High Velocity Innovation. Figure 8.6 shows how this works in the context of the Rapid Learning Cycles framework.

Knowledge Supermarkets

Once you move beyond your first set of programs, the amount of knowledge captured begins to grow exponentially. Knowledge Supermarkets are where a team stores its knowledge for easy reuse. This means that the knowledge needs to be cataloged in a way that allows for both browsing and searching.

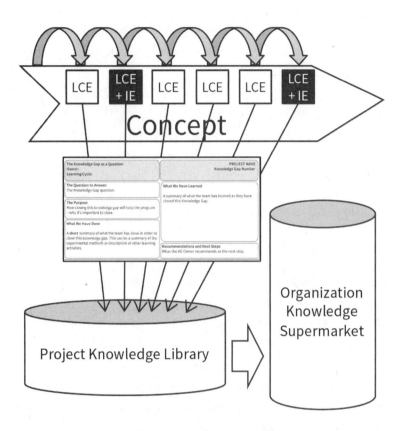

Figure 8.6: Extensible knowledge flow in the Rapid Learning Cycles framework.

The concept of a Knowledge Supermarket doesn't depend upon the tool; I've seen successful examples in file shares and in complex knowledge management tools. The main issue to avoid is overbuilding your Knowledge Supermarket so that you have a lot of empty shelves that don't contain anything yet. It's better to add layers of organization to your Knowledge Supermarket as it grows, so that people can get a full sense of the amount of knowledge the supermarket contains.

In fact, it may be better to first build "knowledge pantries" where teams and functional groups can find the knowledge most relevant to their own work, then organize them into "knowledge convenience stores" before moving into a fully scalable Knowledge Supermarket. If you use modern tools to develop these spaces, there won't be much conversion time.

Finally, as you think about how to get this in place, I found that full-text search quickly becomes useless. Too many things come back that take too long to go through. Establish tagging/keyword standards early, and use these as the basis for your browsing system (but hide anything that doesn't have any documents yet). The sooner you do this, the less rework you'll have to do when you move from one layer of organization to the next.

Position Papers

Position Papers pull an organization's reusable knowledge. This is an idea I saw first at Constellium, the company featured in Chapter Five, and it's become so important to my client community that I've made a simple template available as an A3 Report. Figure 8.7 on the opposite page is a template for a Position Paper.

The Position Paper is a report that reviews the current state-of-the-art for a proposed innovation project. The authors review the library of extensible knowledge the company has captured about the technology, markets, and customer; the platforms it has developed and the NUDs areas that the program will need to explore. The extensible knowledge can be found inside or outside the company; key suppliers may have made advances in their own technologies that the Innovation Program can exploit.

It's not intended to take a long time; the guidelines for my clients are three people, three days, one A3. Once a group tailors the template to reflect the kinds of extensible knowledge that the organization has, completing it becomes the work of a long afternoon working session. Yet this is some of the most valuable time that the team can spend up front. It defines the contours of the Learning Phase of the program and ensures that the team avoided the waste of reinvention as much as possible.

This type of document is also valuable for other types of innovations because it asks the team to capture the current state of the

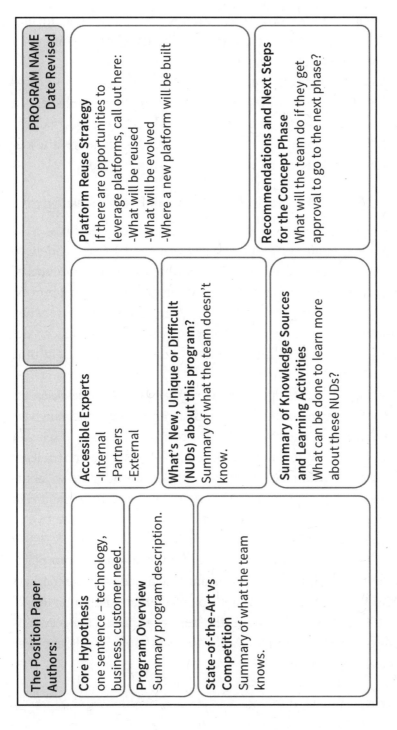

The Position Paper
Authors:

PROGRAM NAME
Date Revised

Core Hypothesis
one sentence – technology,
business, customer need.

Program Overview
Summary program description.

**State-of-the-Art vs
Competition**
Summary of what the team
knows.

Accessible Experts
-Internal
-Partners
-External

**What's New, Unique or Difficult
(NUDs) about this program?**
Summary of what the team doesn't
know.

**Summary of Knowledge Sources
and Learning Activities**
What can be done to learn more
about these NUDs?

Platform Reuse Strategy
If there are opportunities to
leverage platforms, call out here:
-What will be reused
-What will be evolved
-Where a new platform will be built

**Recommendations and Next Steps
for the Concept Phase**
What will the team do if they get
approval to go to the next phase?

Figure 8.7: The Position Paper

knowledge regarding what the organization is attempting to do, including the knowledge available to the team from benchmarking companies that have made similar changes.

The combination of real-time knowledge capture, systems to organize it, and a process for pulling it into new programs establishes the conditions for a team to focus only on the truly NUDs aspects of the program. If your company anticipates the needed knowledge and develop it in advance, that can accelerate innovation even more.

Cadenced Release Plans Pull Extensible Knowledge

If you're in a consumer market where products get released for specific seasons or market windows, you already have a good start on cadenced release planning. Cadenced release plans outline when new products or new product variants will be launched, or when new operational process improvements will be implemented. They help teams anticipate when specific innovation challenges need to be solved so that teams can deliver a continuous stream of innovation to the market at the right time for customers.

Lean Startup advocates developing a regular cadence of releases, especially for software and other services that can turn around new versions as often as every couple of weeks. The concept of cadenced releases is even more important for physical products because you can't release products so frequently. Since launching a physical product is so labor-intensive and development cycles are measured in years, the default is to load every good idea into the next product. After all, it could be two or three years before the team gets another chance.

As the other elements of High Velocity Innovation fall into place, the pace of product releases accelerates until it's timed with the market's ability to absorb a new product. When you reach that point, it no longer makes sense to put every idea into the next new product. Every new feature adds complexity, and the Marketing team can only talk about so many new features at once.

I call this model a "cadenced release" strategy because it flows best for you and for your customers if there is a regular rhythm to the releases. That way, the release plan gains the benefits of cadence that a team experiences with learning cycles: the ability to coordinate work with each other by aligning work with the program's heartbeat and aligning that heartbeat with the pull signals from the market. You, your support teams, and your customers will benefit from a regular rhythm that makes the series of releases seem orderly and manageable instead of chaotic and disorganized.

This approach has many benefits that arise from leveling out the flow of innovation to the market: resellers and distributors always have an exciting new release to talk about, product managers can better focus marketing messages for each release, and manufacturing and supply chain partners have less complexity and risk. The major benefit is that it allows the company to anticipate the extensible knowledge it needs to build into its platforms, so that this knowledge can be built in advance.

You can document cadenced release plans on the Product Roadmaps that I described in Chapter Four, with some slight modifications. First, the releases need to be clearer about the performance targets and features that each release is expected to include, including a forecast of the NUDs elements that will be used for the first team in each release. Second, the Product Roadmap will need to be paired with a Technology Roadmap that shows when this extensible knowledge will be built.

Technology Roadmaps to Build Extensible Knowledge

A Technology Roadmap looks a lot like a Product Roadmap with the same time periods. But instead of market segments or product categories, the roadmap has technology workstreams. For an IoT product, the workstreams might be the app, the cloud-based database, the communications between the device and the cloud, and the device itself, which may have more than one workstream. Figure 8.8 is an example of a Technology Roadmap for a paper mill that has the strategic objective to reduce energy consumption.

Purpose: Define the R & D development needed to reduce carbon emissions and energy consumption.		Technology Development Roadmap to Reduce Carbon Emissions and Energy Consumption in Paper Mills			
Strategic Objective	Top Priority R & D Needs	2019	2020	2021	2022-2024
Reduce Carbon Emissions and Energy Consumption	Reduce energy for black liquor concentration by 50%	Water removal by membrane technology to replace early stages of multiple-effect evaporator: identify membranes with the potential to withstand process conditions.		Develop membrane-based processing equipment	Develop membranes with acceptable performance characteristics and robustness
		Processing technology improvements	Wash medium/fluid improvements to improve process efficiencies		New concepts for separating water from black liquor solids
	Use biomass and other alternative fuel sources to replace fossil energy	Compare and prioritize alternative fuel choices based on performance, availability and cost	Develop processes for acquiring, handling and storing biomass fuels.	Develop model for lime kiln performance including economics, lime conversion and productivity	Develop improved methods to recover and utilize internally-generated solid waste streams as fuel.
					Develop new sources for alternative fuels.

Figure 8.8: The Technology Roadmap.

The innovation leadership team that developed these roadmaps knows they need to have platform teams working to resolve the NUDs aspects of these features in enough time to incorporate them into the Execution Phase for the next program. They can plan resource leveling and build Learning Plans to meet these needs.

There are limits to how much a platform team can do before they have a real product target. Platform teams build theories about features, design elements, and technologies that may be useful in the future. It takes a real product team with real dates to pull the theory into practice. For that reason, the shelf model used to describe this is more like pulling the ingredients to prepare a meal from scratch than pulling a prepared meal from the deli counter that just needs a microwave. Your development teams still need to know how to cook if you want an enjoyable dinner.

Even though they won't be able to complete most of their work until the product team is underway, they will be able to do the most difficult work; and because they didn't know the final specifications of the first product to use the technology, they will be more likely to build knowledge that is more generalizable across multiple products.

Extensible Knowledge Drives High Velocity Innovation

For Sonion, the power of extensible knowledge helped them achieve major reductions in time-to-market for their ideas. As they become more aggressive with their time lines and more predictable about meeting them, they can build stronger relationships with customers and pursue more opportunities. They now expect all of their programs to use the elements of High Velocity Innovation, including a focus on building—and extending—extensible knowledge throughout their programs.

Your Next Actions

☐ Look for examples of extensible knowledge in your own company; you may find it in Engineering, Marketing, Procurement, Production, or anywhere else.

☐ Write a Position Paper for one of your current programs: What knowledge does your company already have? Who are the experts you can draw upon?

☐ If your company has an accessible Technology Roadmap, look at it to identify the levels of extensible knowledge being developed. If your company doesn't or you can't get access to it, sketch one out for your own area of work.

CHAPTER NINE

Hyster-Yale uses a tool that allows them to track whether or not Key Decisions and high-priority Knowledge Gaps were closed on time.

Terry Snapp, Process Leader for Global Product Development, helped design the system configuration that allows them to keep track of progress. At the 2017 RLC Virtual Summit, he said, "Simple good charts show who needs help. If someone has a late Key Decision, I know to check in with that person. They also tell me which Key Decisions were closed late so that I can think through how that will impact the program."

Metrics for a Running Innovation Team to Track

These are the three most important metrics to track in a program that uses High Velocity Innovation.

- Key Decisions Made on Time predict whether or not the program will hit its next milestone on time, and ultimately whether or not it will launch on time. It's also the best measure of how well the leadership team supports

High Velocity Innovation, because they are the decision makers. If they create problems for the team by changing program direction or scope, by not being available to make decisions, or by coming to meetings unprepared to make commitments, this measure will show that.

- High-Priority Knowledge Gaps Closed on Time predict whether or not those Key Decisions will need to be revisited, and also measures the effectiveness of the team's Learning Cycles Plan. When a team is able to close its most important Knowledge Gaps before Key Decisions need to be made, the decision makers are able to make better decisions. If the team focuses on too many low-priority Knowledge Gaps because they're easier to close, this metric will highlight their need to refocus.

- COGS (Cost of Goods Sold) of the Product versus Plan. If your products are targeted at mass production, a dime of extra cost can mean millions of dollars of lost profit. Even if you make 100 percent custom products, any cost overruns hit your business right on the bottom line. You can start tracking this metric very early, so long as your process is clear about the team's level of commitment. This target will float until the point in time when you will commit a per-unit COGS to the business.

These three metrics are the minimum health check that your program needs. But you can get a sense of how well your teams are doing before any of these problems show up in the metrics.

When It's Going Well, You'll Know

I can tell when an Innovation Program is going well when the team is engaged and the events are dynamic. The Innovation Program Leader knows how much to expect from the team, when to push a little, and when to back off. The Knowledge Gap and Key Decision Reports are clear, even to me as an outsider. Teams recognize that they found and defused conflicts that would have taken months to surface with the old system.

You'll start to see the pace pick up as the practices of High Velocity Innovation become more widespread. The team will spend less time revisiting decisions—and asking you to act as referee. Instead, they'll spend more time sharing what they've learned. Their decision recommendations will become sharper, and they will focus their best effort on the aspects of the program that are truly new because they'll be able to leverage the rest.

You will know when your organization is working well. But if something needs adjustment, it will be easier to spot if you have been observing the team, reflecting on the results, and monitoring some carefully selected metrics.

Lead with Observations

When you attend team meetings or walk around your office, you can learn a lot about how well things are going by paying attention to what you observe. These observations are not quantitative metrics. They are leading indicators of the results that will show up in the program metrics if you don't address issues when you see them. It's easier to make adjustments when the team is new and the program is not very far along than it will be to make them later, after team norms have crystallized and the program is in its busiest phases.

Here are some questions to ask yourself as you reflect on your team's progress:

Team Health

- How is the team's general morale and stress level? Are people relaxed and calm, or are they a little frantic?
- Do they seem to be overloaded? How much tension is in the office?
- Do people seem to be working well as a team?

Team Events

- If you are a leader, you may not attend Status Events, but no matter what position you're in, you'll start to hear about them. How are they going?
- Do people complain about how long they are?
- What happens at Learning Cycle and Integration Events?
- Are Knowledge Gaps closing?
- Are Key Decisions being made?
- Do the team members actively participate in the discussion or do they mostly listen passively while Team Leaders do the talking?

Knowledge Gap and Key Decision Reports

- Do the reports share conclusions and recommendations or just data and information?
- How well written are the Knowledge Gap and Key Decision Reports?
- Do they capture what you need to know now?
- Do they capture what you will need to know for the next version of the product, so that you don't have to do the experiments over again?
- Do they contain links to the important backup information?

Sponsorship

- What do you hear from the stakeholders? Are they engaged?
- How much visibility does this program have outside the team?
- Does this program seem to have the priority that it merits?

Effectiveness of the Innovation Process

- What do you hear from the team?
- What do the team members say about the process when you speak to them one-on-one?
- Are they getting used to it?
- Do they like it? If not, why?
- What are the sources of friction for them?

Your Own Experience

- What do you notice about yourself?
- What are your sources of friction?
- Have the High Velocity Innovation practices helped you become a better leader, coach, and partner, or is it making things harder for you?
- How worried are you about the team and the product right now?
- Does it seem as though the team is building the product you have envisioned? If not, why not?

Metrics for Monitoring Innovation Programs

If you don't know where you are, how will you know that you have changed for the better? What does success look like?

Even if you sense that the programs are going well, you need to prove that to the sponsors and business partners who support you and the other stakeholders whom you depend upon to get the product out the door. You need to demonstrate that this framework is an improvement over traditional product development as practiced at your company. You may need to prove to investors that this framework is leading to the product you have promised to deliver.

You are considering High Velocity Innovation because you want something specific: the ability to accelerate your most important innovations. If it's important to you or to your company, you can define metrics around that result, and around other desirable outcomes like better quality or lower costs across all products and product families.

Product Metrics

For product innovations, you need to demonstrate that you delivered a great product. The product is not too expensive to make and does not drain money on warranty repairs and support calls. The product sells well with good market fit and provides the company with a nice profit from each sale.

You can establish some metrics that predict the product's performance. These metrics give you the visibility to make adjustments so that the product will be more likely to hit your targets. In fact, for something like Cost of Goods Sold (COGS), you're almost guaranteed to miss the mark if you don't monitor it early and often.

You may already have predictive models that help you estimate the cost of warranty claims or service calls. For innovation programs, these models are less useful because the degree of the program means that historical data may not be as relevant. But they're still valuable to track even if they aren't as reliable; the magnitude may not be correct but the trend line direction probably is.

Process Metrics

We use process metrics to help us understand the health of the program while the program is running. They generate stronger pull for good results because they are more immediate. You may have delivered a process innovation that can only be measured this way.

Process metrics measure one piece of the overall program in order to predict the outcome of the whole. They can be dangerous because the whole does not equal the sum of its parts. As long as you are able to remember that predictions of success are just predictions, process metrics can help you spot problems quickly.

Results Metrics

Results metrics are important for determining whether the framework has delivered its promised value. But the time it takes to show these results diminishes their power to have any impact on the results.

When reporting an organization's results metrics, it's best to create a bridge between the short-term process metrics and their long-term counterparts for your teams, and then report them both together. This is especially true if you are using the practices of High Velocity Innovation for the first time and want to demonstrate the contribution that these practices have made to your program's success.

The combination is especially powerful because the senior leaders see that they are getting what they want, and the people on the team see the connection to the things they did differently to achieve the results. There are few better ways to ensure that your sponsors and team will be eager to use the framework again.

How to Define a Metric

A metric is an answer to the question, "How will we know that we have succeeded?" The short-term answers become your process metrics, while the long-term answers lead toward results metrics. Ideally, it's not too difficult to gather the underlying data or calculate the metric, and the methodology makes sense to everyone.

A good metric begins with good definitions for its key terms that don't conflict with other organizational meanings. What does it mean to be done? How do you know that a Knowledge Gap has been closed? How do you define the Integration Event? How does your finance department calculate COGS?

A good metric is measurable. Some things, like team engagement, are subjective and therefore hard to quantify. You may have to find a proxy, such as the number of people who participate in team celebrations or you may need to use an employee satisfaction survey.

A good metric is actionable. There is a clear link between the metric and the things people can do to change the metric.

Finally, you will need to develop the mechanism and timing for collecting results. You rarely have existing data to support process metrics, so they will be believed only if people understand how you collected the data and what methods you used to analyze it.

The Balanced Scorecard for the Innovation Program

Some groups establish a long list of metrics, but this just adds a lot of work for your teams without adding much value to the program. You need to be selective about the metrics you monitor. If you are in a process-heavy organization that tends to measure everything, you will need to prioritize the metrics you track.

I recommend that innovation teams use a modified balanced scorecard approach to metrics. As described by Robert Kaplan, balanced scorecards have Financial, Customer, Operations, and Learning & Growth metrics.[1] The scorecard shown in Table 1-1 splits Operations into Product Health and Process Health. I replace Learning & Growth with Team Health because team members learn and grow a lot by virtue of participating in a Rapid Learning Cycles program. Team members' participation in corporate training experiences should be tracked elsewhere.

- **Financial.** The projected and actual financial performance of the product. Process metrics should show that the product is forecast to sell at a profitable price to achieve a good return on investment (ROI). This requires modeling price performance, which depends on the business model, feature set, and competitive offerings. COGS models work best when you establish a cost budget with guidelines and an escalation path for exceeding it.

- **Customer.** The projected and actual customer engagement for the product. Process metrics measure the amount and effectiveness of customer engagement during development, before there is a product to buy. The results metrics capture the number of customers versus the forecast number, as well as their reactions to the product, which are measured by reviews and customer ratings.

- **Product health.** The projected and actual quality of the product. The time taken to close technical Key Decisions is a leading indicator: if decisions get taken late too often, there could be problems with the system architecture or the general approach. The other process metrics measure product quality and how quickly the team can resolve issues. The results metrics all reflect the cost or impact of design flaws.

- **Process health.** The current state and impact of the Rapid Learning Cycles framework. Process metrics help you monitor the health of the framework. Results metrics help you demonstrate that the framework made a difference.

- **Team health.** The current state of team engagement and the impact on team members after the program is finished. The process metrics in this area help you spot problems within your team before they affect the program. The results metrics gauge your team members' reaction to the framework after they have been through one complete program.

In the table, I give two or three sample metrics in each category. Don't try to keep track of them all; if you choose one from each row, you will have five process metrics and five results metrics, a reasonable number to collect without too much impact on your time.

	Process	**Results**
Financial	• COGS Model • Projected ROI • Projected Pricing Model	• COGS versus Forecast • ROI versus Forecast • COGS versus Forecast • Time to Breakeven
Customer	• Customer KDs Made on Time • Customer Validation Results • Beta Test/Early-Look Results	• Unit Sales versus Forecast • Adoption/Conversion Rates • Reviews and Customer Ratings
Product Health	• Technical KDs Made on Time • Percent of High-Priority KGs Closed • Product Validation Test Results • Percent BOM From Platforms for Program Magnitude	• Support and Warranty Costs • Scrap and Defect Rates • Product Return Rate • Percent Platform BOM versus Forecast
Process Health	• Key Decisions Made on Time • Percent of High-Priority KGs Closed • Length of Status Meetings	• Number and Impact of loopbacks versus Similar • Projected versus Actual Move to Production • Time Spent in Industrialization versus Similar

Team Health	• Invitees versus Attendees at Integration Events • Time Lines and Accuracy of KD and KG Reports • Employee Turnover During the Program	• Team Satisfaction/ Engagement Surveys • Requests to Use Framework Again • Employee Turnover, Quarter After Launch

These metrics are only suggestions. It will be better if you ask the question, "How will we know that the program is going well?" and then use these examples to formulate your own metrics, using the words that are most meaningful to your team and stakeholders.

Metrics that Waste Your Time

Some metrics simply aren't worth tracking, even though they might seem like a good idea. Either they either measure things that are not measurable, or the measures encourage teams to do the wrong things instead of the right ones. Avoid the temptation to establish measures such as:

- Raw Number of Knowledge Gaps Closed or Time to Close Them. Teams won't try to close every Knowledge Gap and may find faster ways to close them.

- Detailed Schedule Variance. The activity schedule changes so often, and there is so little visibility into what needs to be done at the beginning, that measuring schedule variance at the activity level is useless. Even the Learning Cycles Plan is too dynamic. If you have to measure conformance to plan, measure it at the level of Key Decisions. Those are the elements that get on the critical path if they are not made on time.

- Time or Money Required to Reach Individual Gates. When you measure how rapidly a group gets to Detailed Design, it encourages them to take shortcuts in the Learning Phases—

and that is exactly what they should not be doing. Using Rapid Learning Cycles will require more time in the early phases, but you will make up that time in late development.

- Percentage Completion of Anything. Activities are done or not done. Knowledge Gaps are closed or open. Key Decisions have been made or have not been made. Major milestones are reached on time or they aren't. Too many projects get stuck in "90 percent complete" for more than a quarter of the total schedule for "percentage completion" to be a useful metric.

Measuring the Pace of Innovation

It's one thing to measure your ability to accelerate innovation with one team, but how do you measure the pace of innovation for an organization? You need both process and results metrics there too. These metrics are especially important because they measure whether or not your leadership team is generating pull for innovation, holding themselves and their teams accountable for supporting innovation. As I described in Chapter Two, companies generate pull for innovation in part by expecting it, tracking it, and making results visible.

Process Metrics

To measure the health of innovation at an organization level, measure whether or not teams have the time and money to be innovative, and measure how they use those resources.

- **Percent of Budget/Resources Devoted to Innovation versus Plan.** This is how you hold leaders accountable for allocating resources strategically versus focusing only on the current business. It's not enough on its own but it is an early warning sign that a manager is prioritizing resources away from the activities that are more future-oriented.

- **Percent of Key Decisions Made on Time Across Programs.** This holds leaders and teams accountable for pulling innovation forward, and also serves as an early warning that innovation teams are not adequately staffed or that support groups are ignoring them.

- **Average Actual Launch Date versus Forecasted Launch at Tool Release.** This measures whether or not you are successfully avoiding the revisited decisions and design changes late in development that cause so many programs to be late. If you are in a market where products must launch on time to hit market windows, this isn't the best measure of innovation effectiveness. In these markets, teams commit unsustainable acts of heroism to get products out on time. Instead, consider measuring the average COGS versus forecast or Engineering change requests post-launch as proxies for the degree of late program turmoil.

Results Metrics

For innovation programs, results metrics focus around the contribution that innovation has made to the business.

- **Percent of Revenue From Innovation Programs.** This is the metric that helped drive innovation at HP, 3M, Google, and many others. It encourages the entire organization to line up behind new products and accepts the fact that innovation programs may cannibalize some existing products; in fact, this metric doesn't penalize teams at all for doing that.

- **Percent Penetration/Adoption in New Markets.** If the need to enter new markets is key to your innovation strategy, then it's helpful to know how successful you were at penetrating that new market. That tells you how effective your teams have been in building customer knowledge and developing compelling products that fit these new markets.

- **Products Released/Cycle versus Planned.** This is a measure of how effective your strategy has been at driving innovation. Roadmaps get updated often; the baseline is the roadmap that was operational when the program was launched. If your average program is a year, you would measure 2020 results against the 2020 plans as defined at some point in 2019.

- **Average Time From Gate One to Final Gate.** This is the core measure of innovation velocity. Gate One is often the first clear milestone for a program and the first major management decision; prior to that, smaller teams work in a much more uncertain environment. In most companies, this is a set of averages based on the scope of the program. Incremental products can get to market very fast, while new platforms naturally take longer. The best way to define this is to look back at the products you released in the past three to five years and organize them into levels of effort, then calculate the average innovation velocity by level. That sets a benchmark you can use to measure improvement.

While these results drive teams and their leaders to make better decisions, other metrics lead teams to focus on the wrong things.

Organization-Level Metrics that Drive the Wrong Things

Organizational-level metrics lead to unhealthy behaviors or unclear relationships between inputs and outputs.

- **Growth Metrics.** Growth metrics, such as unit sales increases, don't tell you very much because there is no link between the growth number and the things you did or didn't do that would foster or inhibit growth. The data is easy to collect, but it's too difficult to interpret in an actionable way. For a single product, all you can measure is your performance against another similar product, or the incremental addition to revenue from new customers.

- **Number of New Patents.** This limits a team's view of innovation toward those things that are patentable. Unless you're in the business of licensing patents, it's not a good idea to let your

IP strategy define your innovation space. Some of your more interesting process innovations may be better kept as trade secrets. Celebrate patents when awarded but look elsewhere for how effectively you're innovating.

Although the ultimate measures of your success are relentlessly objective—revenue, cost, quality, and market acceptance—the best measures to run your program don't require a calculator. They mainly require you to use your powers of observation.

What Do You See?

All of these metrics don't replace your own two eyes and ears. What do you see and hear? What observations do you have? What's not as smooth as you'd like it to be? What's working better than you expected?

When I visit a client site, I like to walk through the team workspaces and visit their conference rooms. I'm usually not looking for anything specific. I just visit the spaces as quietly as I can and ask myself what I notice.

The Physical Space

- What's on the walls or in the conference rooms?
- Are they using visual models to communicate, or a lot of text and numbers?
- Do IT and Legal policies get in the way of the ability to share information? (If the walls are bare, that's usually why.)
- Does it look like they inhabit the space, or is it a bit sterile?
- Does the space support collaboration and creativity?

The Work Environment

- What are people doing when they're not in an event? Are they at their desks working alone, or are they working in pairs?

- Are there a lot of impromptu meetings in conference rooms or the coffee area? Is it a noisy or quiet space? (Either is okay, just different.)
- Does the room seem energized or tired?

Engagement

- What time do people come in, and when do they leave?
- Relative to the company norms, are people eager to get to work?
- Do they stay late? Do they perhaps stay later than they should or work weekends?
- Where do they take lunches or breaks?

Cross-Functional Teams

- How easy is it for non-colocated team members to participate fully in the program?
- Is the audio or video quality okay for remote meetings?
- Does the team manage time zone differences well so that team members don't have to disrupt their sleep?
- Are the key elements of the Rapid Learning Cycles framework—the Logs and Learning Cycles Plan—available online for remote teams to view?
- Has the team had a face-to-face with their remote colleagues?

What Keeps You up at Night?

What are you most worried about right now?

I knew we were on to something special with the Rapid Learning Cycles framework when one of our early adopters, Lone Baunsgaard at Novozymes, told me that she was completely relaxed over the Christmas break; the program was on track and she had nothing to worry about because the team knew where it needed to focus to make the right Key Decisions. She could let go and enjoy the holidays.

If you are not in that space, why not? That probably points toward some hidden Key Decisions or Knowledge Gaps that need to be brought to the surface where they can be closed.

Your Next Actions

- ☐ Find out how your company currently measures time-to-market for new products. If you find that this is not being tracked, review the last three years' programs to get some baseline data for the time from First Gate to Launch.

- ☐ Take a walk around your team's area and ask some questions about what you see.

- ☐ If you are tracking schedule variance for detailed activities for any program in early product development, stop immediately. Instead, track whether or not major decisions and deliverables are getting done on time. Encourage your team to use simple tools to manage their own activities.

PART THREE

How to Build High Velocity Innovation

CHAPTER TEN

EXPERIMENTS WITH HIGH VELOCITY INNOVATION

Part Two of the book covered a lot of ground from high-level strategy to individual Knowledge Gap Reports. In this section, I'll describe the transformation model that will help you go all the way from where you are now to a system that will help you achieve High Velocity Innovation.

You might be in a place where you don't think you can put the entire system in place. You can experiment with pieces of it, and although you won't get all the acceleration your teams are capable of, you will see things get measurably better. That may be enough to build momentum and eliminate the rest of the barriers so that you can do even more.

Dave Berg of Greenheck saw opportunities to use Rapid Learning Cycles to define the spec for a specific application and for plant startups. These types of programs have a lot of unknowns at the beginning, and the decisions made for these programs have long-term implications. They need to be made with a high degree of confidence.

These areas may not seem like the best place for Rapid Learning Cycles because they are not traditional product development programs. But they have both high uncertainty and high cost-of-change. This is the type of situation that is ripe for some experimentation.

Small Steps to High Velocity Innovation

The good news is that you don't have to do everything to start seeing results. In fact, it's better for your teams to run some experiments first with some of the core practice areas that will deliver results right away. That will encourage them to keep trying more and more of the system. When you have enough experience with that, then you can try a pilot program.

Figure 10.1 shows the model that I've guided most of my clients through over the past six years, including many in this book. Each phase of the transformation extends the work done in the previous phase, building on the successes and adjusting the things that didn't work. The model builds momentum for change by leveraging the way that innovative people think: experimenting with new ideas, spreading the ones that work, and eventually consolidating and standardizing where it's useful, but always allowing for the range of activities that fall under the umbrella of innovation.

The Experimental Phase is a natural first step: read the book; try out some of the ideas; see if they work. If so, keep going. If not, stop before you commit the whole organization to something that won't work. After you build enough support this way, you're ready for a full pilot.

The Pilot Phase allows you to prove to even the most hardened skeptics that your company is capable of achieving High Velocity Innovation. Some industries, such as pharma and aerospace, see themselves as being so different that these internal proof points will be essential if you want to get permission to go further. For others, this is a chance for the pilot team to encounter all the gaps you'll need to close before moving ahead.

After launching a successful pilot, a Learning Phase helps the rest of your organization build their skills while a focused team builds out the rest of the system. The Transformation Phase gets everyone through their first experiences. Finally, a Sustainability Phase puts in the needed architecture for this to become business as usual.

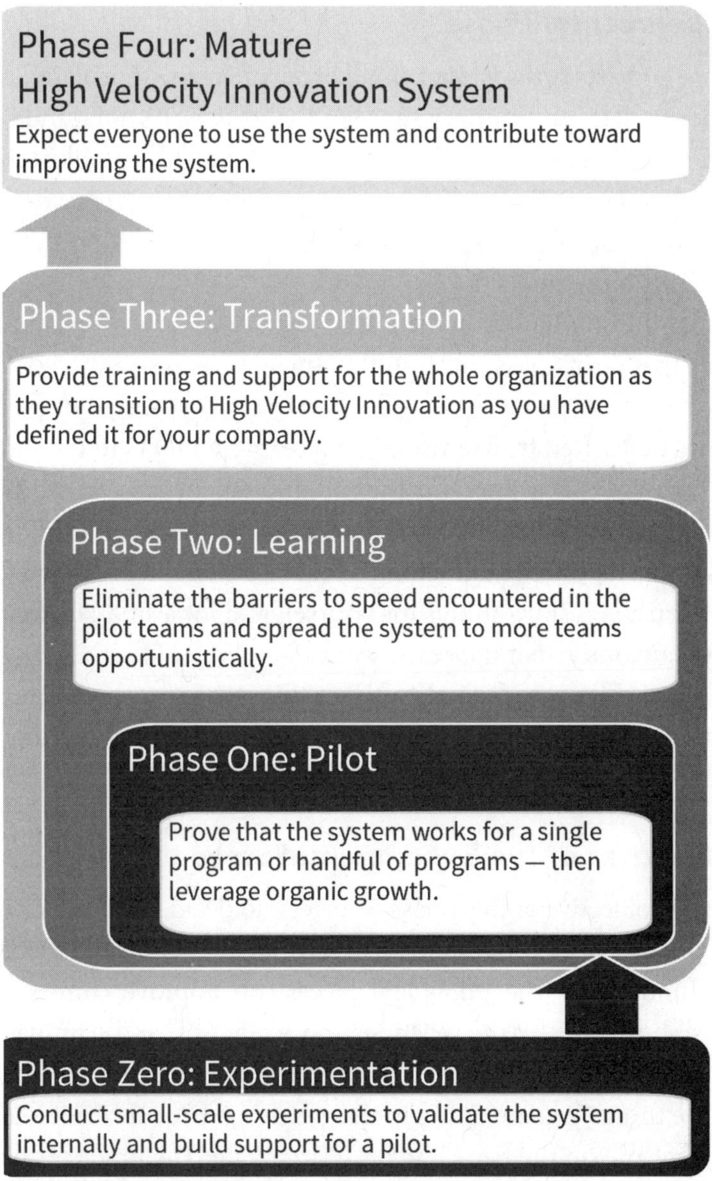

**Phase Four: Mature
High Velocity Innovation System**

Expect everyone to use the system and contribute toward
improving the system.

Phase Three: Transformation

Provide training and support for the whole organization as
they transition to High Velocity Innovation as you have
defined it for your company.

Phase Two: Learning

Eliminate the barriers to speed encountered in the
pilot teams and spread the system to more teams
opportunistically.

Phase One: Pilot

Prove that the system works for a single
program or handful of programs — then
leverage organic growth.

Phase Zero: Experimentation

Conduct small-scale experiments to validate the system
internally and build support for a pilot.

Figure 10.1: How to build the High Velocity Innovation system.

Even if your organization is ready for a complete transformation,
the Experimental Phase can help accelerate your progress as you move
through these other stages.

The Experimental Phase

This phase consists of a series of small experiments with isolated practices in order to get a preliminary sense of the system. It's a natural thing to do, and I encourage readers to do this by providing things like templates for A3-style reports, book study guides, and step-by-step guidelines for running stand-up meetings. You'll find these resources on the website associated with the book.

Among the companies in the Rapid Learning Cycles community, the only ones that didn't pass through this stage were in so much pain from their existing system that they were ready to try anything. But even these companies benefitted from empowering team members to try some specific practices as they waited for the full implementation of the system.

For most teams, this is a casual process of trying something to see if it works. The steps are small enough that you don't need to ask for permission. You can just try things for yourself and for a small team without impacting anyone else if it doesn't work.

Just a little bit more formality about this stage can accelerate a company into a full-scale pilot much faster. That starts with getting much clearer about what you're testing and why.

The Objectives of the Experimental Stage

The primary objective of this phase is for you to decide whether or not you want to run an entire program using the principles and practices of High Velocity Innovation. The individual pieces can improve communication and decision making, make meetings more efficient, and eliminate some of the downstream problems that make innovation programs take too long.

But the things you are doing in this phase are probably not enough to move the needle on the time it takes to innovate. The practices work together and reinforce each other to accelerate innovation in many places. Without this reinforcement, the practices are hard to sustain, and more likely to run into barriers they can't overcome.

Therefore, it's important to keep your expectations and your managers' and teams' expectations low for this phase, and define your experiments so that they deliver meaningful results even if they're small. At the same time, the team recognizes that this isn't sufficient to make them faster across the whole program and that the practices they try aren't sustainable without more support from the organization.

Choose the Right Experiments

If you're in charge, start with things that resonate with you and why. Are you attracted to the idea of speed in general? Do you wonder how well your organization really understands the strategy? Does it seem like your teams waste a lot of time with revisited decisions or long, slow loopbacks during the execution stage? Do initiatives for new products or other types of innovation start and stop and start again?

If you're doing a book study, ask the group which chapters from Part Two resonated, and see what the individuals in that group may be willing to try on their own. Ask an Innovation Program team leader to read this book and then reflect with you on some small steps to get started.

You may want to consider sending one person to a Rapid Learning Cycles workshop to see what they want to try after they get back. That will also help you identify your first pilot program.

These reflections and questions will point toward the areas in which some focused experimentation will lead to big benefits.

Choose the Best Places to Start Experimentation

In general, we want to experiment with teams that are poised to have a good experience right away and are not so far down the process that they'll get frustrated by all the missed opportunities.

This means focusing first on the earliest stages of innovation development: Idea Screening, Advanced R&D, programs that are not yet in a formal phase gate process, or programs that have just entered the first phase. Teams in these early stages often have loose procedures and few hard deliverables. That makes them ripe for experimentation, and the benefits you achieve here will build momentum for a pilot program in the next phase.

It's not a good idea to experiment with groups that are already deep into implementation; if you already committed the tooling budget or moved into upscaling, then it's probably too late. The disruption of having to do something new is just a distraction to a team that is deep into product validation, firefighting, and defect-fixing mode. It's not easy to run a clean experiment.

Run a Clean Experiment

Once you've chosen where to start experimenting, it's important to choose what you are experimenting with. What is your hypothesis for this experiment? How will you know if your experiment succeeded?

Figure 10.2 shows an A3 Report to define an experiment during this phase. This will help you understand what hypothesis you're testing and why, then record what happened and what you decide to do next. If your company is new to A3 Reports, this is one place you can start using this powerful tool to improve communication.

You might try to break down a Key Decision into Knowledge Gaps with this hypothesis:

"By identifying the Knowledge Gaps we need to close to make this decision, we can run the right experiments to develop a better recommendation so that we get a better decision made at the right time."

The measures of such a test would be the number of Knowledge Gaps the team was able to close, the opportunities for learning that they would not have found otherwise, the quality of the recommendation, and whether or not the decision was revisited later.

You can't know for sure if High Velocity Innovation is working until you execute innovation more successfully. But you will be able to get a read on whether or not the team is healthier, making better decisions, revisiting decisions less often, and engaging more effectively with the leadership team.

Here are the kinds of early wins to look for:

- Early warnings about conflicts between functional partners or potential defects that would normally surface later.

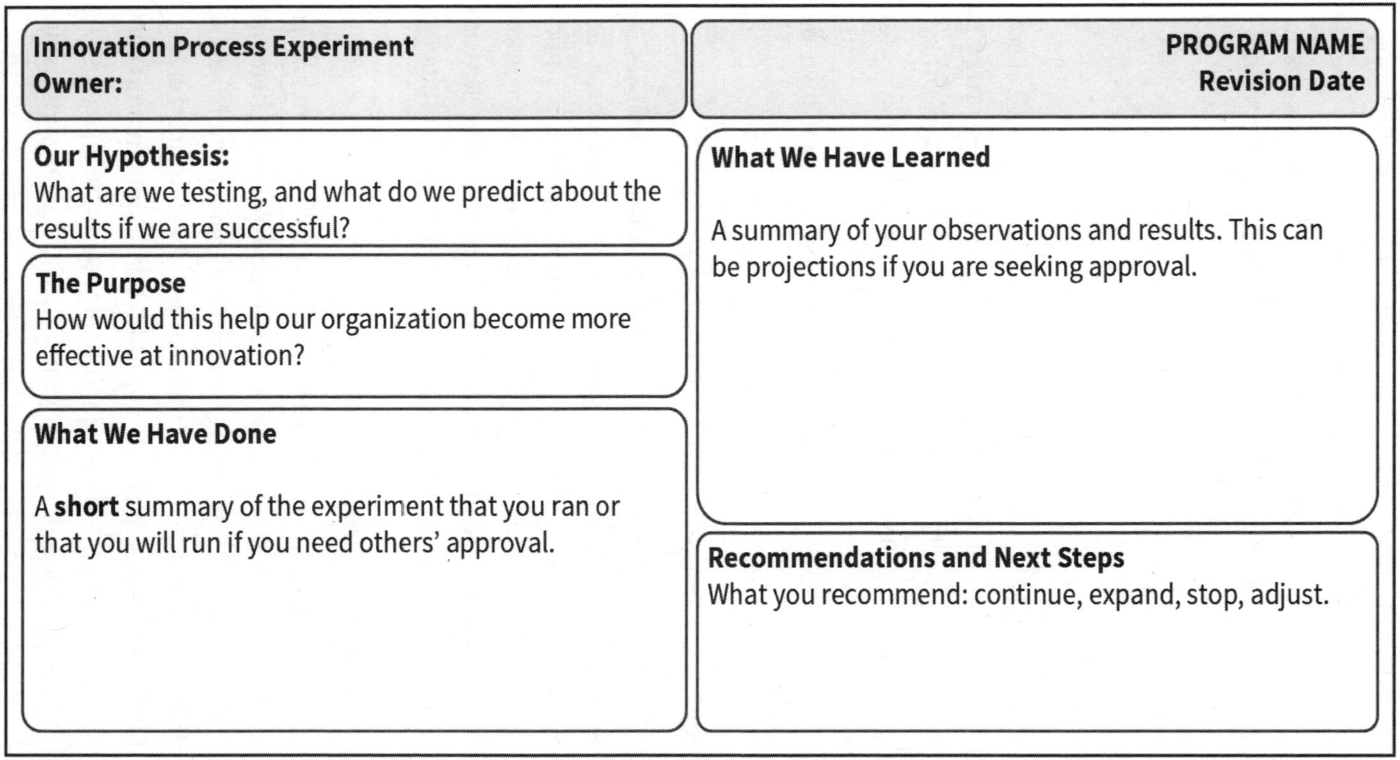

Innovation Process Experiment Owner:	PROGRAM NAME Revision Date
Our Hypothesis: What are we testing, and what do we predict about the results if we are successful?	**What We Have Learned** A summary of your observations and results. This can be projections if you are seeking approval.
The Purpose How would this help our organization become more effective at innovation?	
What We Have Done A **short** summary of the experiment that you ran or that you will run if you need others' approval.	**Recommendations and Next Steps** What you recommend: continue, expand, stop, adjust.

Figure 10.2: The High Velocity Innovation Experiment A3.

- More cross-functional decision making and more collaboration across functions to get things done.

- Clearer agreements with leadership about what the program is supposed to be, and faster recognition when a program has experienced "mission drift."

- Recognition that a decision that would have been made early with limited information needs to be made later with better information.

Berg saw early signs of success by using Rapid Learning Cycles to define the Core Hypothesis for an Applications Engineering program: "What are we truly trying to accomplish?" Then when it was time to write the spec, the teams had greater confidence with less back-and-forth.

You'll accomplish these early wins by implementing your own defined set of practices.

Team-Level Experimentation Practices

Not every practice in this book makes sense for these experiments. Corporate strategy is probably beyond the scope of even the Pilot Phase. You can pull together a pilot team that has a new structure, but that's not a small-scale experiment. Rapid Learning Cycles works best when you put that entire framework in place in the Pilot Phase. Here are some elements for which an individual experiment would deliver meaningful results.

Product and Platform Roadmaps

Product and Platform Roadmaps might seem like odd things for an experiment because the scope and scale are so large. But the experiment here isn't to go through a major strategic planning exercise; the goal is to pull together what you already have into a roadmap, and then see where the gaps are.

If you are on the commercial side of product development and such roadmaps don't exist, then build out a picture of your current state, starting with last year's products, then this year's, then the ones planned for future years. This gives you something to take around to your stakeholders for review and feedback. You'll know it helped if you have better discussions with them about what products and platforms the company needs, and when it needs them. The outcome will help identify the best programs to target for acceleration first.

Core Hypotheses for Programs

Every Innovation Program has a Core Hypothesis. Outside of High Velocity Innovation, few teams know how aligned they are around the same hypothesis, and whether or not the leadership team agrees with them. This is another quick experiment that can immediately improve communication and alignment: ask the team to identify the key customer, business, and technology values for their program, and then write a sentence that contains them all.

The final outcome is much less important than the discussion, and you'll know it worked when the team no longer argues about fundamental questions but instead refers to the Core Hypothesis as the rationale for the learning activities they will undertake.

Major Key Decisions/Knowledge Gaps

This is the type of experiment you can do in any program. Take one Key Decision—one high-impact, high-unknown decision—and break it down into Knowledge Gaps by asking:

- What does the team already know about this decision?
- What do they need to learn?
- What does the decision maker need to hear in the recommendation in order to accept it?
- Who are the other stakeholders who need to be consulted?
- When does this decision need to be made?
- Can we do something to push it later?

This will naturally lead the team to design some experiments or other learning activities to close those Knowledge Gaps. That naturally leads into thinking about the best way to communicate their results. The early sign of success is a confident decision that the team and their stakeholders don't revisit later.

For the Manufacturing Startup program, Dave worked with Kristin, the team's project manager, to help her team identify the Core Hypothesis, Key Decisions, and Knowledge Gaps that were specific to this type of program. That naturally encouraged the team to follow the rest of the process.

A3-Style Reports

Of all the practices in this book, A3 reporting is the one that encounters the most initial resistance until someone gives it a try. Too many people are comfortable with their lengthy slide decks that cover every possible question a decision maker will ask. Yet they are much more likely to get clear decisions from decision makers that can see all the information right up front. A3-style reports help both the report author and the report reader to focus on the most important information.

This is why I like to introduce them early, model them in my own work with my clients, and encourage teams to try them for at least three months before giving up on them. As a leader, writing and asking for A3-style reports is the type of activity that immediately signals your intention to do new things. As a program manager or team member, it signals to management that you want to do your very best work, and you're willing to be innovative in your approach to get there.

For Berg's team, the A3s provided tangible proof that the Key Decisions were solid and could be relied upon. That made it easy to commit to the specs for the specific application.

Metrics

If you don't track some of the high-level metrics described in Chapter Nine, now is a good time to start. In fact, some of my best clients have done a "look back" of the past three years to see how they performed by mining historical data, before starting the work to accelerate innovation. If the numbers are bad, that will help generate momentum for change. If the numbers are good, then you may do well enough, or you could have achieved those results at the expense of something else, usually quality or cost. Establishing a baseline makes it easier to recognize success later, and it may also point the way toward other experiments that will lead to more improvement.

How to Get Started

You thought through what hypothesis you want to test, which practices you want to try, and how you'll know if your experiment was successful. What do you do first?

Buy Copies of this Book to Share

I don't say this to make my publisher happy, but because it's how most of the companies in this book got started. They ran book study clubs with either my first or second books to build a team of people who were eager to try out the ideas.

It's a good way to get others to begin thinking along these lines. It will place the experiments that you run into context for the people who are being asked to do things differently. It will encourage others to run experiments of their own.

But don't just pass out copies of the book. Encourage people to get together to talk about the ideas and take the action steps as a team. What makes sense? What will be challenging? What doesn't seem like a good fit at all?

And most important, where are we now and where can we best get started?

Don't Wait for the Perfect Time—Just Start Somewhere

Is your corporate strategy missing or unclear? Are you in the middle of ramping up production for a big season of sales? Have you just had a major reversal, reorganization, merger, or anything else that could make change even more difficult?

The temptation is to delay the test until a better time. If that better time is days or weeks away, it's okay to hand out books and talk about ideas over coffee until things die down. But if the disruption is major and long lasting, then it may have created enough chaos that there's an opening for experimentation with new things.

That's especially true for reorganizations. They break down the informal networks that people rely upon to get things done. High Velocity Innovation can become the glue that holds the new organization together.

There is no perfect time to start a journey like this. There is always a good reason to stay with the present state.

Don't Expect to Get It Right the First Time

It's healthy for your company to experiment with lots of different things at once. It's also healthy for them to run lots of variations so that you get good information about what works and what doesn't. In fact, that experimentation will only grow during the Learning Phase, when you begin rolling out practices to more teams.

Not all of these experiments will work the first time. You might need to adjust some tools to find a good fit in your company. You may have tried to do one piece, such as Integration Events, which requires other pieces to work well (Key Decisions and Knowledge Gaps). Your organization may not be ready for an A3-style charter document if they've never seen an A3 Report at all.

Don't Do Everything at Once

Since the goal of the Experimentation Phase is to demonstrate enough value for a pilot, the experiments don't have to try to achieve the goals of a pilot program. A handful of small experiments is better than one big one.

What Happens If You Go in the Wrong Direction?

Maybe you tried pure Agile and found that it didn't work for you. Maybe you focused on building an innovation team that didn't deliver anything that could be commercialized. Maybe you had to spin off a skunkworks team that delivered a promising product, which your Sales teams couldn't or wouldn't sell, and now you're wondering if that's the only way to innovate. Maybe your investors are getting impatient with the ROI from your advanced research efforts or your last product totally missed the mark.

If so, the first thing to do is reckon with the past so that you can start building support for a fresh approach. I would encourage you to look at this as an opportunity rather than a barrier.

- You have proof that innovation is important to your company's future, even if everyone is a bit discouraged right now.

- The disruption has made people eager for something that will work better than the pain they are experiencing right now.

- High Velocity Innovation could be the solution to the pain they are experiencing right now, without allowing them to go backward.

Some of the companies in this book went down one or more of these paths before settling on the practices that drive High Velocity Innovation. The pain you just experienced can become the burning platform that helps lead your team to a better place.

As long as the leadership team has not been punitive toward the people who made mistakes or tried things that didn't work, you will be able to adopt High Velocity Innovation faster because people will experience it as a relief rather than a burden. You may need to run some quick experiments, and you may decide to run pilot teams in parallel with a Learning Phase to eliminate the process barriers and replace the practices that didn't work.

The biggest challenge is finessing the transition away from the stuff that didn't work toward High Velocity Innovation.

You Just Ran an Experiment and Learned Something

When I visit a team running a new process that hasn't worked, I say, "You just ran an experiment with (Agile, skunkworks, etc.), and you learned some valuable things. One of the things you learned is that this isn't the long-term solution. But you also learned that you are capable of breaking old patterns and doing things differently. That's valuable, and we can build on that to move your teams away from practices that aren't working, into things they'll probably like better because they work better."

It's especially important to communicate that to your teams. This can be hard if you were the one driving the initiative. The people leading that change will have some disappointment to deal with too. Your organization will watch how you treat them. If you are respectful and grateful for the effort as you are firm in reinforcing the pivot toward new practices, that will help others feel comfortable with experimenting. They'll know they won't get shot if they try something that doesn't work.

Leaders in this situation often worry about how making such a pivot will affect their credibility, especially because the leaders probably have people sitting on the sidelines who hope that this will blow over and they can go back to their comfort zones. The reality is: if things are not working, the organization already knows. A leader builds credibility in this situation by acknowledging that the experiment failed but refuses to give up on the belief that the organization is capable of a much higher level of performance and refuses to back down from the need for change.

In a situation like this, the only true failure is to go back to the way things were and accept the results you were getting with the old system. I hope this book has demonstrated that you don't need to do that.

When High Velocity Innovation Seems Impossible

You may be in a different place, and you may be the only one who sees the need for change. Everyone else thinks it will be impossible because of the culture, the industry, budgets, resource overloading, investors, poor leadership—you name it. In this situation, I encourage people to look for the opportunities to do things within their own control and run them as individual experiments to see what happens.

Sometimes that builds momentum for change faster than anticipated. Sometimes it leads to the recognition that the individual would be better off in a different company. At the very least, these experiments make these individuals more effective in their own work and that can be contagious.

In the meantime, it doesn't hurt to see if anyone else is willing to read the book and think through the questions in the Appendix. It doesn't hurt to break down a decision you need to make into Knowledge Gaps and then see what extensible knowledge you can find or build to close those Knowledge Gaps, or to ask others what they need to know in order to make an important decision with greater confidence.

The Roadmap from Here

After running a few small-scale experiments, you may be wondering what to do next. Across all the phases, the typical order of implementation is:

- Experiment with tools, systems, and metrics.
- Pilot Project Management tools: introduce Rapid Learning Cycles and Agile as appropriate. (That's a lot to do and pulls much of the rest of the system.)
- Strengthen the strategy at the company level. Then cascade that down to products and platforms.
- Reorganize to fit the strategy and decide how to manage platform development.
- Put management systems in place to run platforms well.
- Build a training experience, if your company is large enough to need one, that explains how your teams will implement these new systems and tools.
- Lock down on tools, systems, and metrics.

The next step on your journey is to run one, or at most a handful, of pilot teams to assess how High Velocity Innovation can help your innovation programs.

Berg said, "The RLC process brought everyone together and focused on marching down the same road." The Applications Engineers were more than happy to write the Scope of Work as it emerged from a series of learning cycles. As they moved into implementation, the team used RLCs to ask, "Where do we still have unknowns?"

The Plant Startup teams found that the process of establishing RLCs helped them to uncover important Key Decisions earlier than they would have in the past. This brought more focus on the right Key Decisions so that the plant startups had more confidence in the decisions they were making, and that led to less costly rework once the implementation had started.

Berg said, "I'm encouraging our teams to use Rapid Learning Cycles for not only product or Application Engineering projects, but for any project that has high uncertainty and high unknown." Greenheck has experienced organic growth of Rapid Learning Cycles in areas beyond product development because they've been willing to experiment and adapt as needed.

Your Next Actions

- ☐ Decide whom you would invite to join a book study, then send out an invite to talk about this over coffee or lunch.

- ☐ Choose one small personal experiment that you can run, like using one of the templates to write an A3 Report, and then do it.

- ☐ Choose an experiment that your team can run and then suggest it at the next team meeting.

CHAPTER ELEVEN

THE PILOT PROGRAM

Pole/Zero decided to pilot two small programs as preparation for using High Velocity Innovation on one of their largest programs. Pole/Zero makes military-grade communications systems and tunable filters. When both of those programs came in under cost and ahead of schedule, they had momentum to apply High Velocity Innovation to their next major development program, which includes 90 percent of their Engineering team.

By starting small, they were able to use simple dynamic tools, such as whiteboards, sticky notes, and spreadsheets. The larger program requires more sophisticated tools to manage, but their earlier experience helped them figure out how to best use these tools. Technology Manager Nick Basil said, "One of the biggest benefits has been the regimen of a simple, standard way of documenting things. The single page document has been very beneficial, especially as we add new people to the team."

The pilot program is the place where you can demonstrate the value of accelerating innovation. That speeds adoption by proving that your company can make the practices work for its teams.

The Pilot Program Saves Time

As I've said throughout this book, the things people do to accelerate innovation often slow it down. Failing to run a pilot program is one of those things because it creates a lot of chaos for a lot of people as you learn.

Pilot programs build confidence in the organization's ability to succeed with this new model in three ways:

1. They demonstrate that the practices of High Velocity Innovation work for your teams and build a visible success story.

2. They create demand to replicate the experience so that others can get better results too.

3. They encounter all the roadblocks that all the teams will hit, but because the number of teams that hit the roadblocks is small, you can manually lift the team over them.

This last point is one reason why teams do better if they have even a single pilot team running, rather than diving in. That team will find all the rocks in the road that need to be removed so your innovation teams can go faster.

You might find that your downstream partners object to some of the things the pilot team wants to try; it's far easier to get them to bend the rules for a single program. You might find that your phase gate system drives teams to make decisions at the wrong time; your leadership team is more likely to waive these requirements as an experiment to see if it helps accelerate the program without adding too much risk. You might find that your current development process has too much overhead, and you can identify at least a few things that everyone can stop doing immediately because no one misses them.

Pilot Teams Have Two Objectives

Every pilot team for High Velocity Innovation has two main tasks: get the innovation into execution and demonstrate that this process helps them do that faster. Those objectives must be put in writing and made visible to the team, its sponsors, and its stakeholders. If you use Program Charters, both objectives need to be in the charter.

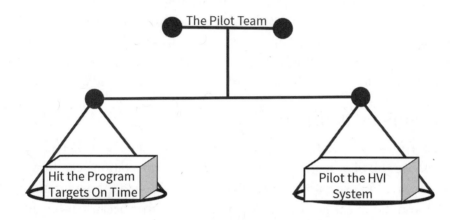

Figure 11.1: Pilot teams have dual objectives.

This protects the pilot team if something like a major redirection causes schedules to slip or causes budgets to get blown. You don't want High Velocity Innovation to be blamed if the team loses three weeks to firefight a customer issue or a customer meeting leads to a reset. If this goal is explicitly stated on the charter or in a similar place, then it will get renegotiated alongside the other objectives if there is a major scope change.

Too often, pilot teams are not able to make their success with new methods visible because their overall program was set up to fail. That gives the naysayers ammunition to shoot down your efforts to go faster when they blame the new methods for making the team fail to meet its original objectives.

If the program is in very early development, it must also be possible for the team to succeed at High Velocity Innovation by helping their program fail faster. If the program's Core Hypothesis is invalidated and there's no good way to pivot, then this team helped the organization make a better decision earlier, and probably saved the group a lot of time and money. That's a good outcome.

When push comes to shove, teams will optimize around getting a new product out the door or hitting critical dates even if this means going back to the way things have always been done. These dual objectives remind the team that for this program, they are just as accountable for how they work the program as they are for getting things done. If a team member hits a critical date by taking a shortcut, which then leads to the risk of a long, slow loopback later in the program, that's a teachable moment for you to request that the work be redone now to defuse this risk.

Planning for Your First Pilot

Unless you know you have the perfect team starting next week, it's better to choose the pilot team, team members, and expectations carefully. A pilot team is an experiment, just on a bigger scale than the explorational work you did in the last phase. The stakes are higher because if the pilot team doesn't do well, you may not get another chance to try High Velocity Innovation methods until the memory of the problems fade.

Choose a Good Pilot Team

It's a mistake to start small by choosing a low-risk pilot program. No one will believe that the method will scale to accommodate the more typical initiative. Instead, it's better to choose a program that the company needs to be successful.

These programs naturally receive more attention from program sponsors, and the program will be more likely to maintain high prioritization for budget and resources. It will be easier for stakeholders and downstream partners to bend their rules for this team because it is important.

Sometimes, the best pilot teams are those that cannot succeed without High Velocity Innovation: the competitive threat that must be addressed, the market opportunity that the team must seize early or lose the advantage, or the breakthrough innovation that customers are clamoring to have as soon as possible.

If you have a similar program and you know that your teams' normal pace won't be fast enough, then you found a great pilot program for High Velocity Innovation.

When the team demonstrates that High Velocity Innovation will work, others will be more likely to see how it could work for their teams, too. Since the program is larger and more visible, it will lead to more opportunities for organic growth. Since the people on the team are more influential, they are more likely to pull the practices into other teams.

Just as with the Experimental Phase, you need to choose a program that is at or near the beginning, ideally entering the first phase of Concept Development or Feasibility. This is where the practices of High Velocity Innovation make the most difference by preventing problems in the Execution Phases. This is especially important for piloting Rapid Learning Cycles. Teams that start Rapid Learning Cycles with a lot of knowledge debt struggle to get off to a good start. If they make Key Decisions too early or without doing much learning first, then they could have a lot of this debt to pay for later in the program.

For Pole/Zero, the two small projects were the right scale for an experiment that they could not have run with their entire team at once.

Choose the Right People

Teams with these characteristics tend to attract your best people: the ones who will be most willing to try a new approach. The majority of people on the team should be aware of what High Velocity Innovation involves and should be eager to try it. One or two skeptics help balance the team, but they should know that active sabotage or grumbling outside the team won't be tolerated.

Junior engineers and scientists can help energize the team. If this is their first experience with a program at your company, they will learn better habits even if the pilot doesn't proceed to full adoption. Marketing, Finance, Supply Chain, Production, and other functional leads need to be senior enough to persuade their peers to give this team room to experiment with new methods.

Give Them Basic Support

You will need to help lift the team over the gaps because the entire High Velocity Innovation system isn't in place.

- **Strategic alignment:** It's possible that your strategy already contains all the elements (described in Chapter Four) to pull innovation from this team. If not, you don't have to get a comprehensive strategy in place for your entire organization. However, you need to get strong strategic alignment for this specific team so that they can build a strong Core Hypothesis. If your company is not clear about why they need this program, it will be hard for downstream partners to be flexible and support the team to succeed as a pilot.

- **Tools and other support structures:** The team may use your IT tools differently than they're used by other teams. They need permission to experiment with doing things differently. The team may also need a visual planning tool or a collaboration tool that they don't have. Your IT group could spend months finding the perfect tool, but you probably don't have time for that. So this team may need permission to start using some new services on a temporary basis while your IT team looks for the ultimate solution that can be brought in house.

- **Metrics:** The team should track metrics from the beginning. You probably don't know what your final metrics will be yet, so you can use some of the ideas from Chapter Nine as a place to start. Determine what metrics will help prove to your colleagues and leadership team that the practices of High Velocity Innovation are delivering better results. What will most help build momentum for the next phase?

Give Permission to Bend the Rules

Pilot teams, by design, encounter all the broken places in the process—the places where your current methods slow down the pace of an Innovation

Program. Decide what's important for the team and then give them permission to ignore the rest. There may be a lot of deliverables that the team decides to ignore.

If you have a heavy weight Product Development Process, you may need to sit down with the team in advance and decide what they will do and what they will not do in order to accelerate innovation. If you work in a regulated industry, you may need to decide how long the group should remain in the Learning Phase before they put their documentation under regulatory control. It might be longer than it is for a typical program.

They'll definitely ask something different from the management teams at the gates: they'll make recommendations and they'll need the management team to accept those recommendations unless there is a compelling reason to make a different one that can be explained to the team. They may give A3-style status updates instead of formal reports. They may track their program schedules on whiteboards with sticky notes and minimize their interactions with enterprise Project Management tools.

They may need to do things at different times. They'll look for opportunities to delay decisions. They may need to purchase some long lead time items before they close on others that don't need as much time. The concept of "design freeze" becomes less like flash-freezing at a point in time and more like the gradual way a pond freezes in the winter.

Your downstream partners may need to do things to lift this team over the gaps that would not be sustainable if every team needed that kind of help. The commitment you need to make is that you will help them this time for this team, and you will work with them to eliminate the barriers or adapt to them if the group moves into full adoption.

Running the Pilot Team

Now that you chose a good team with a good program and put some basic support structures in place, it's time for the pilot team's first meeting.

Start with a Good Kickoff Event

In Chapter Seven, I said that the Rapid Learning Cycles framework begins with a Kickoff Event to build the team's Learning Plan. No matter what elements of the High Velocity Innovation system you intend to use, the team needs to align on what they will do differently. The Kickoff Event is your opportunity to explain the pilot to them, give them basic training on the practices that they'll need to do differently, explain how their progress will be measured, and help them develop the implementation details, such as where they'll put their Learning Plan.

Reinforce Key Documents and Events

The team will immediately enter their first learning cycle and start writing Key Decision and Knowledge Gap Reports. It's a good idea for the Innovation Program Leader to see these reports about a week into the first learning cycle to make sure that team members aren't waiting until the day before to write them. The first reports take more time to write than the ones that follow a bit of experience.

The events should be placed on the team calendar immediately and held to the dates that they are due. This is one of the key ways that High Velocity Innovation generates pull. If you allow dates to slip, especially on the first pilot team, then all of your dates will slip.

At the same time, these are "come as you are" events for people to report what they've learned. Sometimes they learn that their original plan didn't give them any useful knowledge. Team members that attempt to use slide sets in traditional ways instead of writing Knowledge Gap and Key Decision Reports need to be redirected immediately. I've sometimes required an individual to review all reports with me in advance to help them make this transition.

Pull Learning Forward, Push Decisions Later

This is the area that often changes the most. Teams need to make decisions at different times than they have in the past. Since the entire structure of High Velocity Innovation is built on "learn as much as possible up front and then decide what to do later" there will be much more concern for the timing of decisions.

At the same time, your downstream partners are not prepared to live in this world. They still expect the same things from your team, and they'll probably build in the same buffers that lengthen the time line. They won't believe that this works until you prove to them that it does.

Your leaders are used to demanding that teams make decisions because engineers sometimes overanalyze their problems and that seems to slow things down. Once they see what knowledge the team has and what knowledge is missing, they are more likely to see the value in delaying decisions. The team will need to make their Knowledge Gaps visible to reinforce this.

Decide what you can delay and ask your partners what they can decide to delay. The program doesn't have to be perfect to be better; it just has to be more effective. If you can diffuse even a few of the long, slow loopbacks that get in the way, then you'll be far ahead of where your typical teams have been.

Capitalize on Enthusiasm

Once your pilot team is off to a good start and showing early results, other people will perk up and pay attention. If they like what they see, there is no reason to hold them back. Just make sure that these enthusiastic early adopters get the needed training to be successful with whatever tools they want to try. The pilot Team Leaders will be too busy to act as private tutors and coaches for everyone.

Pilot team members should be encouraged to introduce these practices into their other teams. They may want to try slightly different approaches, and this should also be encouraged.

Consider these to be experiments operating in parallel about how to best tailor the practices to fit you. Such organic growth is a sign that the practices are showing promise, and the more internal successes you have, the easier it will be to move from Pilot Phase into full-scale adoption.

Allow for Organic Growth Within Limits

At the same time, you need to give guidance on the things that the pilot teams are allowed to avoid (and other teams must continue to do for now). Your commitment to downstream partners is that you would not overwhelm them with too many teams requesting things that are hard for them.

Teams can and should be encouraged to build Learning Plans but they may need to maintain the traditional concept of a design freeze as your downstream partners expect them. They can (and should) look for ways to learn faster, but they may have to accept that their stakeholders can't move as quickly yet.

Teams may begin to chafe at the restrictions once they know how much better things could be. That drives momentum to get to the next phase, when you'll clear all the roadblocks left in your way.

When Is It Time to Move On?

Most groups don't wait for the pilot team to get all the way through Execution before they decide to move into the next phase. If the pilot program has gone well with solid early results, there is enough pull for High Velocity Innovation that teams are ready to move forward. The teams that started their own experiments will be ready to do more, and the leaders and stakeholders that interacted with the pilot team will be eager to get the same results for their other teams and to interact with them in the same way.

This is your signal that it's time to begin laying the groundwork for full-scale adoption. At Pole/Zero, it was clear that using High Velocity Innovation on their next large program was a logical step. Since that would cover so much of the development organization, it meant they would have near-full adoption by the end. Nick said, "We've gone through several different hurdles to get the team's members to think about things differently."

The under-time, under-budget performance of the pilot programs gave them a powerful incentive to learn how to do that.

Your Next Actions

☐ Identify a set of candidate pilot teams that will enter a new phase of early development sometime in the next quarter.

☐ Talk with the Program Managers to see who would be open to running a pilot, and encourage them to begin experimenting with the ideas on their own.

☐ If you are an Innovation Program Leader or engineer who would like to be a pilot, your next action is a little different: start sharing the ideas with your management team and look for a willing sponsor to support you in running a good pilot.

CHAPTER TWELVE

HIGH VELOCITY INNOVATION AT SCALE

When I began working with Keurig in the fall of 2017, the group had already passed through the early phases of their transition to High Velocity Innovation. In fact, they had already transitioned most of their teams into a new organizational structure and started using Agile methods for program management. Some of their early experiments worked; others had unintended side effects. During my first visit, I spent a lot of time talking with people about what they experienced so far and worked to develop a plan that would pull them the rest of the way into full adoption.

Since I started working with Rapid Learning Cycles in 2010, I had been down this path with more than a dozen other companies, including Novozymes, Constellium, Sonion, Hyster-Yale, and Gallagher, whom you met in earlier chapters. Not everything we tried worked, but the results these companies achieved gave me confidence that Keurig was in a great place to go beyond the Pilot Phase into full-scale adoption.

When you've seen enough and are ready to bring the benefits of High Velocity Innovation across the organization, it's time to prepare for full-scale adoption, which takes place in three different phases.

The Learning Phase

First, you'll take advantage of organic growth and remove the biggest rocks that will get in the way of full-scale adoption across teams. The purpose of the Learning Phase is to figure out what High Velocity Innovation looks like in your organization in the long term. Your pilot teams have given you some valuable experience to show where your organization will struggle when every team is working this way. You can start to tune your systems to address these potential roadblocks.

At this time, you'll give your teams some basic training on Rapid Learning Cycles and establish the other elements of High Velocity Innovation. Your teams will interpret this guidance in different ways, which creates an opportunity to strengthen your systems. Every team's interpretation becomes an experiment that will give you insights into how your system can be strengthened.

You don't have to do this alone; it's better to treat this like an Innovation Program and build an HVI team. Pull together a cross-functional group, including people who lived through the pilot team's experience, people who may have picked up the practices on their own, the person who owns the PDP or other process that needs adjusting, and perhaps someone from HR. But keep them focused on helping your people "act their way into a new way of thinking" rather than burning a lot of cycles on culture change. The culture will change when people are doing things differently. Figure 12.1 shows the people engaged in a program to drive High Velocity Innovation.

Maybe you have run one pilot team or a handful. They tried to implement the system to the best of their ability, but that doesn't mean their choices were always the right ones or that there aren't better alternatives. For the first six months or year of full-scale adoption, your teams will try lots of different things. Some of them won't work very well, and teams will switch to better implementation tactics. Others will work so well that you'll want all of your teams to do the same things. Your teams are running a lot of experiments in parallel.

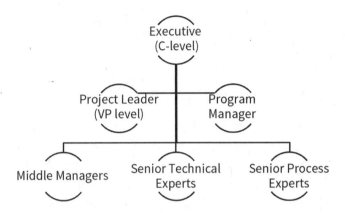

Figure 12.1: The High Velocity Innovation team for the Learning and Transformation Phases.

It is tempting to start standardizing too quickly, before these experiments have a chance to play themselves out. But there is no shortage of other work that will lay the groundwork for sustainable adoption.

Focus Areas in the Learning Phase

Your High Velocity Team will will work to establish the rest of the High Velocity Innovation system by taking the following steps:

- **Strengthen your corporate strategy's ability to pull innovation.** If your leadership is weak in this area, you need to put a "good enough" strategy in place for your organization and then use it as the basis for your first-pass roadmaps. You can validate, iterate, and strengthen it from there.

- **Reorganize your innovation teams as new programs come online.** If you had a separate innovation team, look there to see if you have any potential Innovation Program Leaders who can mentor others on how to close Knowledge Gaps during the earliest phases of development. The other team members can have roles within the product development or commercial business that match their skill sets as the existing programs wrap up. Staff new programs with cross-functional teams of people from your technical and commercial groups who see their participation as time limited and who expect to stay with the program through execution.

- **Begin to build out platforms if you don't already have them.** Decide who needs to participate in platform development, and get those efforts underway by looking for cross-program opportunities to build shared knowledge. Build a "good enough" Platform Roadmap to give these teams a place to start. If you're new to this, the first step is to inventory the extensible knowledge you have and figure out where your major gaps will be. In this phase, platform development work will probably need to be done during the development of specific products. What will change is the recognition that such work needs to be done so that it can be packaged for leverage in the future.

- **Revise your Product Development Process and any other processes for executing innovation to achieve high velocity.** Review the lists of required deliverables for every new product and major process change to make sure that they all add value in the new system. Ensure that Gate Review expectations and decision criteria are flexible enough to allow for designs that freeze over time instead of a flash-freeze on a specific date. Encourage teams to delay Key Decisions until the last responsible moment and require them to use the tools (Rapid Learning Cycles, Agile, traditional Project Management) that fit the phase and nature of their work without constraining how they interpret the tools.

- **Get the leaders the training they need too.** Leaders need to come to Integration Events and Gate Reviews prepared to give useful feedback and guidance that reinforces the system of High Velocity Innovation that you're trying to build. This means that they can't ask for deliverables that don't make sense in this system, such as Gantt charts for the activities in early product development. They can't take decision making authority from a team once it is delegated to them, and they must be prepared to listen to the knowledge and information a team has developed to support a recommendation before rejecting it because they don't like it. They need to come to meetings when they're scheduled or find an alternative way to give feedback, rather than expect teams to fit meetings around them.

- **Define a small but meaningful set of standards and documents that all teams must follow and provide templates for them.** Key Decisions are not made until Key Decision Reports have been written and approved. Knowledge Gaps are not closed until the Knowledge Gap Reports have been written and accepted by the team. Learning Cycle and Integration Events take place as scheduled and do not move. The organization may establish a standard learning cycle so that these events sync up, which makes it much easier for leaders and team members who support multiple programs.

- **Put systems and tools in place to support sustainability and growth.** Unless your company is very small, you'll probably want some kind of virtual visual planning tool. You'll need a place to build the first version of your Knowledge Supermarket. You'll need to start tracking metrics to establish a baseline against which you measure improvements.

- **Help your downstream partners prepare for full adoption.** As the number of teams you move into this new system grows, so will the impact on downstream partners. The pilot teams have showed you where the issues are; now you need to help them attack these challenges so that when you move into full adoption, they are able to keep up. If they're used to working in serial, you'll need to help them figure out how to work more in parallel. If they're not usually asked for feedback or to close Knowledge Gaps of their own in early development, they may need some help to figure out how to contribute effectively and how to balance this with work on the current business. The good news is that High Velocity Innovation works by reducing the churn that typically occurs when an innovation moves into execution, and all the risks turn into realities. The pilot teams' experiences should have shown them that teams that work this way are much easier to work with, even if they do things a little differently.

This is a long list of things to do. At this point, "done" is far better than perfect. Even the best, most experienced people I've ever worked with don't get everything right the first time. Companies and industries differ in the best way to implement these details, and there is always some trial and error in this phase.

Additional Pilots in the Learning Phase

Small- to mid-sized companies outside of regulated industries can start to transition the rest of their teams to High Velocity Innovation in these phases because the system-level barriers are more inconveniences than true roadblocks. Others will expand the pilot program pool to cover more of the organization's complexity: additional geographies, business units, or product categories.

The regulator of your ability to scale is the capacity of your downstream partners to absorb the impact. They're still in a place where most of the programs they encounter have a lot of problems in late development. They may need some time and assistance to think through ways to shorten lead times, relax interior constraints, and build new relationships with suppliers that allow for delaying decisions and pursuing multiple alternatives. Once they see how much easier it is to work with a team that has greater confidence in the team's decisions, they will get more engaged.

Even if you can't transition every team, it's still important to capitalize on enthusiasm and allow teams to experiment with those system elements that don't impact other groups. Encourage everyone to share their discoveries with the High Velocity Innovation team and with their other teams. Each person that has had a little experience with Knowledge Gap Reports or rapid prototyping techniques is a person ready to move to the next phase.

The HVI Training Experience

If all the people in your company do not fit in one large room, then one key outcome of the Learning Phase is a training experience that captures your best understanding of High Velocity Innovation as practiced at your company. This too will be a first pass based on your experiences in these last two phases. Expect it to change once you're at full scale and uncover the remaining barriers to adoption.

The training experience is a key part of this because if your organization is big, the majority of people will have heard rumors of the early work you've been doing to drive High Velocity Innovation. The experience is an opportunity for them to learn about the system as you understand it, and wrestle with the principles and practices that are new. It gives them a chance to start the process of figuring out what the new system means for them.

In the next phase, you'll deliver this experience to everyone from the CTO down to the technicians.

The Transformation Phase

The major outcome of this phase is a shared understanding of the need for High Velocity Innovation, a common vocabulary for the elements of the system that you are adopting, and mastery of the new skills your teams need to make this work. By the end of this phase, you'll be ready to put the final elements in place that drive sustainability and accountability.

Training to Build Familiarity and a Common Vocabulary

The purpose of training in this phase is not to magically transform everyone into expert innovators. Only experience and coaching can do that. The purpose is to establish a foundation of knowledge that makes it easier for experience and coaching to build skills and better judgement. Common vocabulary makes it possible for teams to share the results of their process experiments with each other, and for one person to work to the same expectations across multiple teams. They'll practice a few key skills in the training, perhaps A3 Report writing or finding Key Decisions and Knowledge Gaps. They'll internalize these lessons when they're confronted with the need to do it for one of their programs.

I prefer to train teams when they are embarking on a new Innovation Program. That's a teachable moment because you can help teams establish their first Learning Plans and practice skills with examples taken from their new program. If that's not possible, the next best alternative is to train functional peers together: all the Mechanical Engineers in their subsystem groups, all the Electrical Engineers, all the Test Engineers and Technicians, etc. I definitely include a separate training for Leadership, from the CTO down to first-level managers who don't directly contribute to program teams. I also include a training for commercial partners from Sales and Marketing, and for Supply Chain and Production partners.

It sounds daunting but the team driving High Velocity Innovation can divide up the work, teaching specific topics or trading off on doing the trainings. You may not be a professional trainer but your enthusiasm about the subject and knowledge about the company will go a long way to make up for it. Even when I'm the one doing the training or one of my affiliates delivers it, it works best to partner with someone from inside the company who can answer those questions and address concerns from an insiders' perspective.

Variation Across Groups

The variation that characterized the Learning Phase will only increase as you expose more teams to these ideas and they struggle to interpret them for their own programs. If your company has tried other things and then abandoned them, especially if your leadership team has the reputation of pushing the "flavor of the month," then the easiest thing for everyone is to keep their heads down, use the methods that have always worked in the past, and pay lip service to the change.

The way to demonstrate that you're serious this time is to be relentless. Look for every opportunity to recognize and reward the people who are willing to try, even if they don't succeed. Ignore the naysayers altogether; don't praise them for heroics that weren't necessary or reinvention that was more expensive than it needed to be. Give them no attention at all.

Teams that have tried things that don't work should be encouraged to look to their peers for better ideas. The HVI team can serve as coaches and mentors to help people make connections to others facing similar challenges. By the end of this phase, you'll be ready to eliminate the variations that don't work and hold people accountable for using the variations that do work.

Accountability with Patience, Respect, and Grace

Up to now, the change has been limited to the pilot teams and others who were pulled in by a desire to get better results and enthusiastic support for change. Now you're moving it into a population that may not have even been aware of the need to accelerate innovation. Just as the Learning Phase included a lot of experimentation among different teams who were eager to try new things, you now have a group of people who may not be as well informed about what you're asking them to do differently.

You're asking people to make a big change in how they think and act around innovation. Your teams need safety in order to navigate this change. They will make mistakes. They'll try things that won't work. They'll be so focused on the new questions they have uncovered that they'll miss something the old system made obvious.

You're also allowing some time—but not too much—for the more skeptical members of your team to sit and watch. Some people, perhaps including some of the most deeply knowledgeable people you have, may choose to sit on the sidelines for a while. Some teams will be in the midst of a major effort, like building a new plant or absorbing new personnel from a merger and won't be able to make the change as fast as others that have more flexibility.

As long as they are not actively sabotaging your efforts, and as long as they don't undermine the HVI team with constant criticism, it's okay for them to finish up their current projects without changing over to the new system.

A Little Patience Goes a Long Way

Often, a little patience will cause them to move on their own, sometimes becoming the system's biggest long-term champions. Eventually, it will become impossible for them to continue, and then they will have a decision to make about their own futures. But not yet.

Once your system has stabilized, you can hold people accountable. For some who didn't pay attention the first time, you may need to offer some retraining. Others will realize that they just don't like working in this new way, and they would prefer to work elsewhere. And some, but probably only a few, will be asked to leave, but only when you're ready for final cutover.

If this makes you wonder if you'll have a lot of deadwood floating around causing problems, think about this: give people a year to get on board. Tell them that this is not blowing over and you are not giving up, but you are going to give them some time to grow into their new roles and learn how to meet new expectations. After that, you'll have a decision to make and so will they.

Downstream Partners Adjust Slowly Too

In the Pilot Phase, you gave your pilot teams permission to try new things and told your downstream partners that you'd help them shoulder the burden of any unintended side effects. In the Learning Phase, you worked with your downstream partners to mitigate the impact through process changes as more teams began to use the system. As you move into full adoption, your partners need to be prepared for this new way of working at full scale.

They will also try ways to accommodate this change that may not always work the first time. They may have plans that work when five teams use High Velocity Innovation but that breaks down when twenty teams use the system. This is another area where patience, giving the benefit of the doubt, and helping people act their way into a new way of thinking helps to break down barriers.

The Move Into Sustainability

Once everyone has been trained and had a little time to "shake down" the system, it's time to decide what, of all the things that have been tried, you will hold people accountable for. You've been collecting metrics to help evaluate which of these experiments succeeded. The final phase places the remaining pieces to make High Velocity Innovation the way that things get done:

- **Performance expectations:** You've been tracking metrics and now it's time to hold teams accountable for meeting higher expectations and improving these metrics.

- **Process guardrails:** You've experienced a lot of variation to learn which implementation tactics work best; for the sake of your downstream partners, it's now time to pull in the variation with clearer expectations about how your teams will implement the practices and interact with your partners.

- **More aggressive time lines:** By now, you know how much time you can expect to save in the backend of your process because you're doing better work in the front end of the process. But chances are your program plans haven't reflected this, and because knowledge work expands to fill the available time, you're hitting these dates but not coming in early. Now it's time to revisit whether or not you need all the prototype runs you needed in the past, or if you can work even more in parallel with downstream partners as you move toward production.

- **More investment in platform development:** One good place to reinvest the money you save from less churn in the Execution Phase of innovation is to strengthen the platforms teams use as the inputs to their innovation programs.

- **Strategic objectives:** The ability to go faster and to be more predictable has given your organization new capabilities. How can your company make the best use of these new strengths to go after better, more ambitious opportunities?

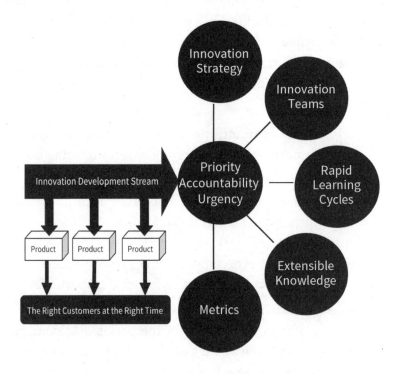

Figure 12.2: A mature system for High Velocity Innovation.

These elements build sustainability and avoid the sense of "flavor of the month" from everyone who first got on board in the last phase.

Figure 12.2 shows what a mature system for High Velocity Innovation looks like. Clear strategic direction, Rapid Learning Cycles, and metrics build a culture of accountability and urgency to pull innovation. Attentiveness to customers and markets generate better product/market fit.

The HVI team sometimes needs to be reminded that they may have worked on this for years but the majority of the organization is still relatively new and inexperienced. It will still take a little longer for High Velocity Innovation to become as engrained as it is at Gallagher or Sonion. Eventually you'll have your own High Velocity Innovation stories to tell.

Take a Break to Celebrate, Then Get Back to It

When you hit the milestone that every team is using HVI, I hope you celebrate it. Take time to recognize the early experimenters and pilot Team Leaders, the HVI team members, and your organization for staying the course through this transition to a new level of performance.

The HVI team can continue working to improve how their company uses the HVI system, continue building skills and bringing new people on board, and share the results of new experiments. For the HVI system to become engrained, it's helpful to keep these changes small and reinforce everything you just taught. Use the metrics to identify instances of backsliding or areas where there is still a mismatch between the process you envisioned and the process they need.

How Long Will This Take?

Every corporate change initiative is unique but there are some patterns I use to predict the time it takes to see measurable results across all programs. If your company ranges from one hundred to 250 people and you're in a market that pulls innovation on an annual cycle, then I would expect your transformation to take about two years (two full product cycles) before it stabilizes.

If you're smaller, already have experience with Agile in some form, or already have good platforms and reusable knowledge, it can take less time—just a year after the conclusion of your pilot program.

If your organization is bigger, you're in a regulated industry that requires a lot of process documentation, or the pace of innovation is slower, then it will probably take longer than that, but no more than three years. It's hard to sustain momentum for a program that takes much longer. If you think this is a multiple-year effort, see if you can break up the work to reach stability faster by, for example, driving things to completion in one business unit before expanding.

How to Know You Achieved High Velocity Innovation

I enjoy visiting the clients who have taken this journey with me. Their teams may not be executing every aspect of the system perfectly, but it's clear that they are much more confident about their ability to innovate. That confidence manifests itself as more ambitious plans for innovation programs, more aggressive time lines that challenge the teams instead of stressing them, and better relations with their major customers.

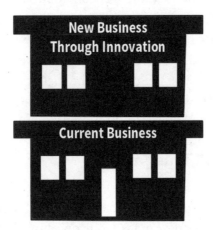

Figure 12.3: High Velocity Innovation builds on strengths to grow new business.

Figure 12.3 illustrates that the mature system helps you grow new business while resting on the foundations of everything you already know about your business, customers, and technology. Unlike the models from Chapter One that have not been shown to deliver results, this model allows innovation programs to be supported by the rest of the organization, with a strong connection between them to ensure a strong flow of ideas and experience from the current business to the new and back again.

Starting back in the Learning Phase, you probably started to see early signs of progress: a program team that met their schedule and budget targets for getting an innovation to market, or an Innovation Program that was killed after its Core Hypothesis was invalidated. When you fully implement the system, these exceptions will become the norm, and then expectations from your business partners and yourself will be higher.

In August of 2018, Keurig celebrated the one-year anniversary of their transformation with a string of product success stories, showing how HVI practices had moved out of experimental mode to spread across all new programs, and how the practices had helped pull teams through the choppy waters of early development.

At this meeting, Roger said, "We've been on quite a journey in the last year but it doesn't end here. We're already working to keep getting better."

Your Next Actions

It may seem like you won't need the material in this chapter for some time, but there are things you can do immediately to start building your company's path.

- ☐ Start tracking baseline metrics, if you haven't already. This is where you get proof that High Velocity Innovation is making a difference.

- ☐ Begin looking for opportunities to work in parallel with downstream partners to delay major decisions and then execute those decisions quickly.

- ☐ Begin building relations with people in other functional groups, divisions, or regions who could become members of the implementation team.

CONCLUSION

I freely admit that I didn't invent the concept of "Rapid Learning Cycles." The phrase first appears, as far as I can tell, in a small book called *The Lean PD Skills Book*, self-published in 2004 by Dr. Allen Ward of the University of Michigan.[1]

Dr. Ward was one of the original researchers into Toyota's Product Development Process, alongside his more famous colleague, Jeffrey Liker, author of *The Toyota Way*.[2] Then Mark Swets and Tim Schipper of Steelcase expanded on this idea in their book, *Innovative Lean Development*, published in 2010.[3]

Pull for Rapid Learning Cycles

Starting in 2011, a series of client engagements pulled the Rapid Learning Cycles framework together. These clients were in different places and different industries, but they all shared a strong commitment to innovation and a determination to develop better ways to bring their ideas out into the world. The people who worked with me during that time are still some of the best people I have ever worked with—innovators who pulled my best work through their commitment to excellence.

Because I was under strong NDAs with all of them, I couldn't directly share the insights or leverage the specific materials from one team with another. They didn't even know the names of the other companies I visited until they saw presentations from those companies at a conference I organized twice a year and saw visual models that looked familiar.

I had to build my own platform of extensible knowledge underneath the insights I gained. Those insights helped me build a fundamental theory of the Innovation Process. I could pull from that knowledge to meet each client's specific needs just as Sonion pulls from a common platform of scientific knowledge about sound technology to produce different microphones for each client.

Four Clients Generate Strong Pull

In the spring of 2011, I joined Tim Schipper on a project for Steelcase to develop a comprehensive training program in Lean Product Development. By then, I had already developed my own platform of extensible knowledge: a set of training materials that I developed for licensing to companies for projects like this. Rapid Learning Cycles appeared as a foreshadowing in that training; some of the foundation pieces had started to emerge but the framework wasn't even a blueprint.

The following year, I accepted a challenge that was completely new: adapt Scrum for an Advanced Research & Development group at Novo Nordisk, a Danish pharmaceutical company that I featured in my first book. Since then, my sponsor, Tine Jørgensen, had been looking for an opportunity to work more closely with me and this looked like a good fit.

I knew Scrum well from my days as a Software Engineering Manager, but it had been years since I had practiced it. I reached out to Kathy Iberle, a former colleague from my days at HP, to help me. It was clear that Scrum had some potential but it would need heavy adaptation, and Kathy had stronger ties to the Agile software community. We visited the team at Novo Nordisk's offices in Gentofte on the outskirts of Copenhagen.

Just as Steelcase was ramping down, another client in Michigan started ramping up. Christian Gianni, then Vice President of Engineering and Technology at Whirlpool asked for my help to build a Lean Product Development training program for 4,500 of their engineers.

Rapid Learning Cycles Between Denmark and Michigan

I spent the fall and winter of 2012 and 2013 flying back-and-forth between Denmark and Western Michigan, sometimes without stopping at home in Portland. In Michigan, I helped the team at Whirlpool develop an architecture for their Lean Product Development program, with a team led by Roger Johnson. As part of this process, we ran some pilot projects using Learning Cycles, but I wasn't satisfied with the results.

In Denmark, I split my time between Novo Nordisk and a biotech company, Novozymes. At Novo Nordisk, Kathy and I supported the research group as they worked out how to apply Scrum. Their experimental work had longer time scales and didn't have the clean outcomes of software development, so it took a lot of adaptation. This project was going very well; I was astonished at the group's creativity and determination. Some of the adaptations they made gave me a lot of ideas about how to help Whirlpool get better results with learning cycles.

At Novozymes I was tasked with helping a team led by Carsten Lauridsen to improve innovation on a number of fronts, including the development of a new process for managing the earliest phases of product development. It was there, at a conference center in Lyngby outside of Copenhagen, that things began to come into focus.

The Framework Pulled Together

I introduced the idea of learning cycles to this team, and I also shared some of the ideas that had been percolating in my mind about adapting Scrum to strengthen this idea. The key insight from this session was that the learning cycle on its own wasn't enough. One of the project leaders, Luise Erlandsen, drew a picture that showed two nested cycles: an inner "learning cycle" on a fast cadence and an outer "Review Cycle" on a longer cadence. I took that picture back to my office in Portland and stared at it for a long time during the holiday break.

In January of 2013, I invited Kathy to come to my office for a working session. I hoped to pull these pieces together into something that would solidify these insights and experiences into an actionable framework that would help all of these clients. Together, we drew the first version of the image that became the stacked circle logo of the Rapid Learning Cycles Institute and designed the outlines of the framework as it is known today. We coined the terms "Key Decisions" and "Knowledge Gaps" in that working session and laid out the event structure we still use today. That day, Kathy said, "If this works, it's a breakthrough."

How to Validate a Breakthrough

In 2013, that was just a hypothesis, but one that we could start testing. Kathy validated it by refining the system in Novo Nordisk's research group, as I ran my own experiments at Whirlpool and at Novozymes, where Carsten Lauridsen sparred with me to challenge and strengthen the framework. Both companies ended up incorporating Rapid Learning Cycles into their Lean Product Development training programs, and I began introducing this framework to other companies.

By 2014, I was convinced that the Rapid Learning Cycles framework was a breakthrough as I watched team after team exceed expectations for cost, quality, and time. Not every program succeeded, but in those cases, I insisted that we follow up to understand what had gone wrong and use those insights to strengthen the method so that others would have an easier time.

But there were two lingering problems: first, aside from my work with Rapid Learning Cycles, Lean Product Development was not growing and seemed to cause more confusion than anything else. Second, I was starting to see a lot of people coming to us who were struggling with Agile for Hardware Development, looking for solutions.

The Right Product/Market Fit

The final problem to solve was a positioning challenge. We needed to pivot away from Lean so that we could leave all of its baggage behind.

We needed to embrace the Agile roots of the framework so that we could reach people who were considering Agile for hardware, before they developed the problems we had seen.

By 2015, all the core elements were in place and I wrote the first edition of *The Shortest Distance Between You and Your New Product*, then began teaching public workshops to get this framework out to a broader audience. Meanwhile, my early adopters were growing beyond Rapid Learning Cycles, and I began working with them on the rest of the High Velocity Innovation system. Their experiences have built the system that I've shared with you.

What Will Be Your Innovation Story?

You might have bought this book because something in the title or description reached out to you, or maybe because someone recommended it to you. Or you might read it along with a group of companions, meeting to discuss the ideas.

No matter where you are in your company, there are things you can start using from this book immediately. Whether you're in a leadership position, or you picked up the book because you're frustrated with your project team, I hope you have some ideas for how to get started.

Other things will take more time, more resources, and more investment. The best way to build support is to start writing your own success stories.

What are you going to do next to get your best ideas to market faster?

APPENDIX A

Book Study Guide

Many of my clients have benefitted from book study groups to help them make positive changes in their Innovation Programs. They either organized or participated in a book study group that got together regularly to discuss a reading from one of the books available about innovation and product development.

If the idea of High Velocity Innovation intrigues you, but you're not sure how the framework would work inside your company, a book study group can help you understand how the framework would need to be modified in order to meet your needs.

For my clients, these groups helped create momentum for change by providing the participants with some time to reflect upon the new ideas they found in their book and to explore ways that the ideas could help their organization. Often these study groups led to individual experimentation with the practices, and then to pilot teams and ultimately organization-wide programs.

How to Use This Book in a Study Group

Here are the steps to establish a book study group in your company:

- Make a list of people who could join you, then ask if they would be interested. Look for people who naturally seek to improve how the organization does its work, and who are willing to experiment with new ideas. List more people than you need (at least fifteen).

- Ask them whether or not they would be interested in reading this book as part of a study group. Include a link to the Amazon page for this book, or the supplemental website at https://highvelocityinnovation.com where you can download a Book Group Study Guide with reflection questions.

- Once you have at least six people, schedule the first meeting and order the books. If everyone says yes, you may end up with too many for one group. Break it into two or more smaller ones if more than twelve want to join you.

- Schedule a conference room that has at least one flip chart for taking notes and a whiteboard. Chapter reviews should not be so formal that they require a projector.

- At the first meeting, pass out the books, and agree upon the meeting schedule, reading assignments, chapter report assignments, group ground rules, and expectations. You may decide that the group will keep discussions confidential, will not bring laptops, etc. Set the rules you need to make sure that the meetings stay focused and on track.

- Take action right away if someone misses more than one meeting so that the group doesn't lose momentum. As the organizer, it's your responsibility to check in when people go missing. If the group isn't working for someone, it's better to let him or her go gracefully so that everyone else is not distracted by the absences.

- After you finish the book, hold one final meeting to reflect upon the group's experience. They may want to tackle another book, or they may want to take some group action to put the ideas into place.

- Celebrate! Do something special to bring the group to a good conclusion.

Best Practices from My Clients

People who have organized book groups shared with me a number of ideas about how to run these groups effectively.

Keep Reading Assignments Short and Focused

There is no way to sugarcoat this: book study groups are extra work. Even if you have a powerfully motivated group, it's important to keep the assignments bite-sized. Not only does that make it easier to get the readings done, it also makes it easier to reflect and internalize the things you learned from the reading as the group discusses them. In this book, one chapter per session will be about right.

Keep Chapter Reports Informal and Discussion Based

Don't assign a book report on every chapter. It is helpful to assign someone to facilitate the study group meetings, but he or she should summarize the main ideas on a flip chart and then generate some discussion questions for the group to consider.

Meet Regularly and Attend Each Meeting

These groups thrive on consistency and a regular cadence of meetings. They can be weekly, every two weeks, or monthly, depending upon how intensely the group wants to work together. Being human, some people will read the assignment the day before the meeting no matter how much time there is between them, and others will read the whole book because it's interesting.

These groups fall apart when attendance is inconsistent or people come unprepared. Erratic attendance drains away the group's momentum, so members need to commit to every meeting unless there is a true emergency or they let group members know in advance that they have a conflict. They need to have done the reading when they arrive.

Keep the Group Small and Closed

These groups help build momentum because they help create strong re-lationships and a shared base of experience among a group of potential High Velocity Innovation leaders. That starts to break down once the group gets larger than twelve, or if group membership changes too often. Close the group to new members after the first three meetings. Larger groups can be broken down into small ones, and latecomers can be en-couraged to organize their own.

Make the New Ideas Actionable Together

Each meeting can end with the commitment to take action, either indi-vidually or as a group. The actions might be to test out one of the ideas from the book, to spend some time observing the organization, or to identify and eliminate an obvious source of unnecessary waste. They don't have to be large actions to get the ball rolling. Small ones add up.

After You Finish, What Next?

At the companies I talked with, book study groups enlisted product de-velopment leadership, recruited and supported pilot teams, built and delivered training programs, and mentored others in problem-solving skills.

Chances are, your own group will develop lots of ideas for next steps and will start to experiment with some elements of the High Velocity In-novation system. When you are ready to run a pilot team, someone from this group will be the best prepared to serve as the Innovation Program Leader.

I encourage you to keep the group together as an advisory board to help shape your organization's next steps with High Velocity Innovation. The group may not need to meet as often. By now, you should know which members are fully on board and which ones are still skeptical. The enthusiastic supporters keep you going and the skeptics keep you honest.

APPENDIX B

High Velocity Innovation teams have a few specific needs for tools to help them work better together. As long as these basic needs are met, the simple tools work better than systems that over-complicate things for the teams.

The Infrastructure to Support High Velocity Innovation

High Velocity Innovation is highly collaborative, and yet strives to minimize the amount of time that people spend in meetings. This means that teams need a way to:

- Track their progress in a visual way that keeps team members, sponsors, and stakeholders informed about the status of the program with as little Project Management effort as possible.

- Make rapid prototypes and conduct quick experiments that push the boundaries of knowledge for their areas of innovation.

- Find the existing knowledge so that they can focus on the aspects of the problem that are truly novel.

- Capture what they learn as they learn it, so that knowledge transfer to downstream partners becomes easier and sharing knowledge across teams becomes easier.

- Manage the formal documents that communicate detailed decisions to implementation partners, such as CAD models, drawings and purchase orders for product development, process maps, work instructions, ISO documentation, and policies for process innovation.

There are many ways to manage all of these things and some of them don't have anything to do with opening up a laptop.

Key Documents

These are the key documents that a team will need to manage.

- **A3-style reports:** In Chapter Eight, I described this powerful tool for improving communication. For many of the teams that I work with, and for their managers, switching to this type of report has been a game-changer. The only piece of infrastructure you need is a printer capable of handling A3/tabloid-sized paper. You can use this type of report to replace almost anything that was previously written in a document or a slide deck:
  - Knowledge Gap Reports
  - Key Decision Reports
  - Position Papers
  - Gate Reviews
  - Design Reviews
  - Process Documentation Summaries
  - General problem solving

- **Short white papers:** If a concept won't fit on an A3, the next best thing is a short (under five pages) white paper. I should be able to read it in less than fifteen minutes. If it's longer than that, only a new hire will take the time. Most people won't bother.

- **Learning and execution plans:** In the beginning, your High Velocity Innovation teams will have visual Learning Plans that can be managed in a variety of ways. As they move into implementation, they may need support from tools that they can use to create Gantt charts of the activities that need to be done. These tools should be as simple as possible, tracking only major activities and deliverables at the program level, while individuals manage their work to accomplish the deliverables.

- **Decision Logs and event minutes:** The team won't track every decision as a Key Decision, so they need a place to put the others that rise to the team level but not to the level of writing an A3. Decisions shouldn't be kept in event minutes, but it is a good place to summarize the team's progress and follow-up items.

These key documents can be placed anywhere the team and its stakeholders can access them.

Real-Time Collaboration Tools

These are the tools High Velocity Innovation teams use most often, even if the team has global distribution.

- Whiteboards and markers, flip charts, paper, pens, and pencils
- Digital camera (a phone/tablet camera is okay), scanner
- Printer and scanner that can handle A3/tabloid printing and scanning
- Masking tape or poster putty
- Sticky notes in a variety of colors
- Permanent markers for writing boldly so that words can be seen at a distance

The physical tools support real-time, face-to-face collaboration, and the digitizing tools make it possible for you to share such work with remote team members.

If you're trying out High Velocity Innovation for the first time, especially Rapid Learning Cycles, then it may make sense to run your first pilot program using sticky notes on a whiteboard. It's hard to automate what you don't yet fully understand. Chances are, the tools you have at your disposal for building a Learning Plan are designed for either Agile or traditional Project Management and will need heavy adaptation. That's hard to do the first time.

The advantage of working with real paper is that it's easier to learn how the system works when you're moving all the sticky notes yourself. It's easier to see the changes when you watch that sticky note move from Point A to Point B. After you've had some practice with this, then implementing online tools will be much easier.

Online Tools

It's possible to run the High Velocity Innovation system with a simple file share. As long as all team members can get to the same location on the server or in the cloud, this is a perfectly good way to collaborate. But a robust collaboration tool gives the team a lot more options.

Collaboration Tools

Collaboration tools such as Microsoft's SharePoint and OneNote, or cloud-based collaboration systems such as Basecamp and Confluence provide the team with a website to which they can post documents, keep track of basic tasks, and start conversations. Revision control keeps track of the latest versions of key documents. Search functionality makes it easier to find them.

Teams can keep their Key Decision and Knowledge Gap Logs in these tools, then link the Key Decision and Knowledge Gap Reports to these records. This makes it easy to navigate among these reports during Learning Cycle and Integration Events. These tools have the ability to store metadata about documents, such as revision date, author, and keywords that make it easier to leverage the knowledge that they contain.

Product Data Management and Configuration Management Systems

Occasionally, I find someone who works in an entrepreneurial setting without basic tools to track product knowledge and deliverables. For software, Configuration Management Systems maintain the official versions of software in development. Check-in and check-out functions provide both conflict avoidance and traceability. Branch paths support iterative development.

Product Data Management Systems do the same thing for hardware. They manage the Bill of Materials (BOM), keep track of supplier agreements and key communications, support workflows for reviewing and approving drawings, and process diagrams and provide a home for complicated models.

Most corporate R&D groups already have tools like this, but they are often lacking in small companies because they used to be cost-prohibitive. Today, there are some good cloud-based solutions that are appropriately scaled for the entrepreneurial team. This should be something that you have and use, but not something that you have to spend a lot of time maintaining.

Knowledge Supermarket Systems

An ideal Knowledge Supermarket keeps track of a few key pieces of metadata about each knowledge capture document, without restricting the format of the document itself. Rapid Learning Cycles teams use Knowledge Gap and Key Decision Reports to capture their knowledge. The system should be able to accept these reports as they are, asking only for the metadata required to properly categorize them.

A good Knowledge Supermarket allows for both browsing by topic and by keyword search. Full text searches sound great in theory but provide too many hits in practice. With keywords, the author decides when the document shows up in searches—and when it's not relevant.

Right now, the most robust Knowledge Supermarkets use some kind of Wiki-like software like Confluence that allows project teams and functional groups to build pages with links to Knowledge Gap Reports, Key Decision Reports, Position Papers, and other documents that capture knowledge.

Virtual Visual Management Systems

When I first started working with Rapid Learning Cycles, the online tools for building Learning Plans weren't flexible enough. Since then, some great tools like Jira and LeanKit have become good alternatives if you must use virtual visual planning.

Be aware that these systems are not easier to maintain than sticky notes. It will take much more time for the Program Manager and the team to manage their workflows with tools like this. It takes just a moment to write a new sticky note and put it on a visual board. The tools enforce metadata requirements that allow for better reporting at the cost of slower data entry. Moving a sticky note from one place to another is also much easier than doing it in the tool.

The main reasons to use such a system are the ability to get better reports to support metrics data collection and the ability to make the plan visible for a distributed team. Even there, snapshots and spreadsheets are fine substitutes for complex tools. In any case, don't jump into this area too quickly. No matter how you configure your system, you'll get a better result if your team works offline before you try to build the online system.

Tools to Avoid

These tools get in the way of doing Rapid Learning Cycles because they were built in the old paradigm of traditional product development. If you can't avoid them without violating corporate policy, minimize the amount of time you spend on them and the amount of data you store in them.

- **Requirements Management systems:** These systems are built around the waterfall paradigm of defining requirements up front and then putting them under heavyweight change control. If you must use a system like this, load the requirements into the system but use placeholders for your Key Decisions. Delay finalizing the requirements that are driven by Key Decisions as long as possible. If you are measured on this, you will need to get permission to take a different approach, or you will spend way too much time explaining to people why you are not defining requirements before the team is ready to commit to them.

- **Knowledge Management systems:** Most enterprise Knowledge Management systems are too elaborate and complicated to store your team's knowledge. Your team needs to access its knowledge quickly and control access to it. The Knowledge Management systems that we have seen are overbuilt. They have been shown to work in industries that rely upon shared knowledge, primarily large management-consulting firms. Those firms may try to sell you a Knowledge Management System, but you probably need a much simpler solution, at least until you have a lot of content to organize.

- **Enterprise Project Management systems:** These systems are dangerous for product development. They give senior managers the illusion of certainty, when really the plans they view through such a tool are much more complex and dynamic. If you must use such a system, store only your Key Decision sequence in there and keep the Knowledge Gaps and activities out of it. You might choose to keep some of the standard deliverables on the plan if that helps your team remember to do them. The time you would normally spend within this system is time you will spend with your team's Learning Cycles Plan and Activity Plans that change too often to put into a system like this.

- **Email and chat systems:** There is a lot of great extensible knowledge buried in email where it can't be found. Chat/IM systems are even worse because they're not intended for long-term storage of information. It's fine to use these systems to agree on where to go for lunch, but not for making project decisions. High Velocity Innovation teams can't afford this knowledge loss. Enforce the use of Key Decision and Knowledge Gap Reports, or ad hoc A3 Reports for things that aren't formally on the plan.

- **Slide presentations:** The bullet-point style works well for things like keynote addresses, trainings, and sales pitches, where they support an engaging (hopefully) presenter who uses the bullets as riffs, and where the actual content behind the slides doesn't have to be completely retained. Innovation Programs are not like this; the ideas that are being presented need to have some meat behind them. This is especially true in the beginning because the way we fight fuzziness is with tools that force clarity and specificity.

- **Lengthy white papers:** Advanced research and innovation groups go to the other extreme too. They try to capture everything they learned in a format that makes their work much more difficult to retrieve later.

- **Team rooms or war rooms:** It's a great idea to give a major project its own space; however, realize that most of the time, the team will use it for meetings and then work back in their own spaces. They mainly need a place to put their Visual Plans, which could be the backside of a row of cubicles, a hallway, or a window with an unattractive view.

Start with What You Have

If this is your first experience with High Velocity Innovation, don't buy anything. Don't buy a Virtual Visual Planning System or a smart board.

Get waivers so that you can avoid Requirements Management, Knowledge Management, or Project Management systems (or at least minimize your contact with them).

Instead, settle on a simple collaboration system that allows the team to share documents as easily as possible. You can probably build this out of the tools you already have or that you can get via cloud-based systems.

Most corporate R&D environments already have some repository to keep product knowledge and software code secure. If you are on your own, this is the one thing to get before you do anything else. If you already have established your repository, and developed good habits for using it, it will be much easier to add new people to your team as you grow.

APPENDIX C

PILOT PROGRAM GUIDE

If you are an Innovation Program Leader who has decided to use the High Velocity Innovation system for your next program, this section includes a checklist to help you get started.

This checklist assumes that you will pilot Rapid Learning Cycles as part of the High Velocity Innovation system, as described in Chapter Eleven. If that's true, then my second book, *The Shortest Distance Between You and Your New Product*, describes this method in much more detail than I could do in this book. You may also want to consider attending a public workshop from the Rapid Learning Cycles Institute to learn more about how to set up Rapid Learning Cycles in the most effective way.

Don't Wait for Your Pilot Team to Get Started

Chapter Ten has some ideas for small-scale experiments you can run while you wait to get your team together for its first Kickoff Event. It would be especially helpful to experiment with Key Decisions, Knowledge Gaps, and A3 Reports because you will work with them every day during the program.

In Chapter Eleven, I mentioned that pilot teams have two objectives: deliver the innovation and test the new Innovation Process. Begin working with your sponsors and other stakeholders now to get aligned on both of these objectives. If you need to negotiate waivers from your leadership team or the PDP Process Owner, do it now.

Finally, plan to pilot this just for the next phase of your PDP. That will help everyone scope their work and expectations, from the leadership team to the individuals on your team. By setting some boundaries, you're able to run a cleaner test of the new process, and your team members will not be asked to answer questions that are too far in the future for reliable answers.

Kickoff Event Checklist

- Identify the people who will be on your team for the next phase.

- Schedule the date for the Kickoff Event. Allow for a full day for a new team, even if the program is small. You'll need extra time to discuss how you're going to do each step.

- Book the location, ideally off-site but at minimum in a large conference or training room with a lot of wall space. You need extra space for subteams to work in small groups, and a blank wall large enough for your Learning Cycles Plan, even if you will convert it to a virtual plan right after the meeting. The best rooms are square, with space for subteams to sit at square or round tables. A U-shaped configuration with movable tables is the next best alternative. Small conference rooms with one narrow table don't work very well.

- Ask everyone who will attend the Kickoff Event to read *The Shortest Distance Between You and Your New Product* before they arrive at the event. It will be helpful (and necessary if you purchased the ebook) for each team member to have his or her own copy of the book. I don't say this to sell more books. When team members have questions between events, they need to be able to get back to the source material. If you have more than ten people on your team, you can send a message to me through the Rapid Learning Cycles Institute, and I can help you with a corporate discount.

Use the resources available at the Rapid Learning Cycles website to develop your detailed agenda, outline agenda, and supplies list. Make sure you have whatever supplies you need to attach things to the wall in the room you have booked. You may need pushpins, T-pins, masking tape, or poster hanging dots. You'll need at least one full pad of flip chart paper; sometimes this is the hardest thing to find.

- Designate a location for your team's Learning Cycles Plan. If you're going to use a virtual visual planning tool, build a mock-up to see what adaptations you'll need to make.

- Customize the templates for the Learning Cycles Plan, Key Decisions Log, and Knowledge Gaps Log by adding your company's logo, your team's name, and your company's confidentiality notices.

- Purchase supplies. If you have to order them, make sure they will arrive at least a week early in case there are problems.

- Order food and drinks for the lunch and breaks. Teams lose a lot of momentum if they have to go to the company canteen or an outside restaurant for lunch.

- Send an email to the participants a week before the Kickoff Event and remind them of the need to read the book, but ask them not to prepare or bring anything else.

- Finalize the timings and structure of the final agenda.

- Hold the Kickoff Event.

Make sure that each team member leaves the Kickoff Event knowing these things:

- When and where the events will be

- What Knowledge Gaps will start during the first learning cycle and who owns them

- What Key Decisions will be made at the first Integration Event and who owns them

- Where the team will put Key Decision and Knowledge Gap Reports

- Where to find the templates for these reports

The First Learning Cycle

Post the Learning Cycles Plan in its designated location, and post the Knowledge Gaps and Key Decisions Logs to the team collaboration site no more than twenty-four hours after the event. The failure to do this has caused more problems with teams new to Rapid Learning Cycles than any other mistake.

Hold your first Status Event as planned, allowing some extra time for adjusting the plan.

Begin your second Status Event with a reminder of the Status Event rules, then monitor yourself to ensure that you are a good model.

By the third Status Event, your team will be off and running, with your first Learning Cycle Event coming up. Now is a good time to check in with each team member to review progress on the first Knowledge Gaps. Ask to see a first draft of their Knowledge Gap Reports. They should be able to fill out the left hand side of the report, even if they don't have any results for the right side.

The first Learning Cycle Event often leads to a major adjustment to the plan. This is normal, because the team will have had one learning cycle of experience closing Knowledge Gaps. They'll probably identify some things that got left off the plan, and other things that aren't as important and should be removed.

They'll also have a much better sense of how much they can get done in one learning cycle. This will probably require them to remove some of the lower-priority Knowledge Gaps from the plan to avoid overload. It's better to focus on closing the highest-priority Knowledge Gaps thoroughly than it is to spend time closing a lot of Knowledge Gaps that are less important.

How to Sustain the Rapid Learning Cycles Framework

The most important thing you can do is to maintain the cadence. If the team decided on two-week cadences, then every two weeks, you'll hold a Learning Cycle Event. All the reasons why the team may not want to hold the event (they're not ready; they got pulled off on another project; a lot of team members came down with the flu) are reasons why they need the event to reset their plans.

The moment you allow any of these events to slip for any reason, all the events start slipping. There is always a good reason to delay the event, especially if people treat these like program reviews where they have to make themselves look good.

Instead, help your team to understand that these are "come as you are" events. They are intended to help the team make adjustments and course corrections as new information comes in. That requires surfacing issues and problems early, while they're small. For some groups, this is a major shock at first, especially the first time a team member has to share "bad news" at an Integration Event.

You can support your team through this transition by watching your own reaction to bad news, and by prepping your stakeholders to help them adjust their reactions to bad news. In my experience, this bad news will surface eventually; hiding it only makes it worse. When you can receive this news with gratitude for the advance warning, and when your stakeholders can do the same, you create a place where teams can be honest about their progress, which makes it easier to see the things that are getting in the way.

Support Organic Growth

As Rapid Learning Cycles becomes embedded in your team and it starts to move smoothly, chances are that other teams or other people will want to get in on the action. If you're not careful about your commitments, you can end up supporting too many teams.

You can offer to facilitate a Kickoff Event or two now that you've done one of your own. You can help troubleshoot Learning Cycles Plans for other programs. But your primary objective is to demonstrate that Rapid Learning Cycles works for your program.

Capitalize on enthusiasm by encouraging teams to find other ways to experiment that don't require as much support. When your group is ready to move into the Learning Phase and support more programs, the people who run experiments are the natural leaders for these new programs.

FURTHER READING

Resource Materials for this Book

Visit https://highvelocityinnovation.com for resources including:

- Examples and templates for the A3-style reports shown in this book, and other key documents.
- Book Study Guide with reflection questions.

Books by the Author

The Shortest Distance Between You and Your New Product: How Innovators Use Rapid Learning Cycles to Get Their Best Ideas to Market Faster, 2nd edition, 2017.

This book explains the Rapid Learning Cycles framework from Chapter Six in detail, with chapters on the Core Hypothesis, Key Decisions, Knowledge Gaps, the Learning Cycles Plan, and what happens inside the learning cycle. It's the core reference book for this program management framework.

The Mastery of Innovation: A Field Guide to Lean Product Development, 2012.

My first book described the experiences of nineteen companies with Lean Product Development. The chapters describing Steelcase, Philips Electronics, Buckeye, and Vaisala proved to be influential in developing the Rapid Learning Cycles framework and the rest of the High Velocity Innovation system.

Other Books for Innovators

Blank, Steve. *Four Steps to the Epiphany: Successful Strategies for Products That Win,* 3rd Edition. San Jose, CA: K&S Ranch, 2013.

Cooper, Robert. *Winning at New Products: Accelerating the Process from Idea to Launch,* 3rd Edition. New York: Perseus Publishing, 2001. e-Book edition location 723–752.

Cross, Stuart. *The CEO's Strategy Handbook: How to Create, Sustain and Accelerate Profitable Growth.* London: Global Professional Publishing, 2011.

Kelley, Tom, with Jonathan Littman. *The Art of Innovation: Lessons in Creativity from IDEO, America's Leading Design Firm.* New York: Currency Books, 2001.

Lafley, A. G., and Roger L. Martin. *Playing to Win: How Strategy Really Works.* Harvard Business Review Press, 2013.

Lockwood, Thomas, and Edgar Papke. *Innovation by Design: How Any Organization Can Leverage Design Thinking to Produce Change, Drive New Ideas, and Deliver Meaningful Solutions.* Wayne, NJ: Career Press, 2018.

Meyer, Mark H., and Alvin P. Lehner. *The Power of Product Platforms: Building Value and Cost Leadership.* New York: The Free Press, 1997.

Nonaka, Ikujirō, and Hirotaka Takeuchi. *The Knowledge-Creating Company: How Japanese Companies Create the Dynamics of Innovation.* New York: Oxford University Press, 1995.

Osterwalder, Alexander, Yves Pigneur, Tim Clark, and Alan Smith. *Business Model Generation: A Handbook for Visionaries, Game Changers, and Challengers.* New York: John Wiley & Sons, 2010.

Ries, Eric. *The Lean Startup: How Today's Entrepreneurs Use Continuous Innovation to Create Radically Successful Businesses.* New York: Crown Business, 2011.

NOTES

Chapter 1

1. Randall, Tom. "'The Last Bet-the-Company Situation': Q&A With Elon Musk." *Bloomberg News*, July 13, 2018. *www.bloomberg.com*
2. Ohnsman, Alan. "Tesla Model 3 Production Stuck In Neutral As Company Rolls Out $2,000 Price Cut." *Forbes*, January 2, 2019. *www.forbes.com*

Chapter 3

1. Cooper, Robert. *Winning at New Products: Accelerating the Process from Idea to Launch*, 3rd edition. New York: Perseus Publishing, 2001. ebook edition location 723–752.

Chapter 6

1. Poppendieck, Mary, and Poppendieck, Tom. *Lean Software Development: An Agile Toolkit*. New York: Addison-Wesley Professional, 2003, p. 57.

Chapter 9

1. Kaplan, Robert S., and Norton, David P. "The Balanced Score-card—Measures That Drive Performance." *Harvard Business Review* 70, no. 1 (January–February 1992): 71-79.

Afterword

1. Ward, Allen C. *The Lean Product Development Skills Book.* Ann Arbor, MI: Ward Synthesis, 2002, p. 62.

2. Liker, Jeffrey K. *The Toyota Way: 14 Management Principles from the World's Greatest Manufacturer.* New York: McGraw-Hill, 2004.

3. Schipper, Timothy, and Mark Swets. *Innovative Lean Development: How to Create, Implement and Maintain a Learning Culture Using Fast Learning Cycles.* New York: CRC Press, 2010, pp. 31–39.

ACKNOWLEDGMENTS

Thank you to the members of the Rapid Learning Cycles Certified® Professionals community who are so generous with their insights and willingness to share with their colleagues, especially Meaghan Carmichael, Karen Cavoretto, Celia Cheng, Bruno Chenal, Vaas Conradie, Jason Cheetham, Peder Fitch, Chris Leigh-Lancaster, Jason Low, Ravi Shehani, Terry Snapp, Suzanne von Egmund, Wouter von Essen, and Justin White.

This book would not have been possible without the people there at the beginning of this journey. Roger Johnson, Christian Gianni, Jeff Williams, Prakash Jayarama, Sugosh Venkataraman, Kurt Heidmann, Tim Schipper, Wendy Hoerner, David Battey, Jamie Payne, and many others helped me experiment with these methods in Michigan. Tine Jørgensen, Anette Sams Nielsen, Mattias Hansson, Carsten Lauridsen, Lone Baunsgaard, Luise Erlandsen, Anders Ohmann, and many others worked with me in Denmark. Kathy Iberle knows my work better than anyone else and continues to contribute to the system's development today.

My early readers helped me shape this book into a coherent structure. I appreciate their dedication, and their feedback was invaluable in shaping the final work. Shivaun Black kept the office going while I closed my door for hours, making sure bills were paid on time and workshop registrations were processed.

I receive encouragement daily on how to grow into my best self so that I can make a better contribution to the world from my companions, especially Mary Jo Chaves, Terry Cappiello, Nancy Pyburn, Linda Smith, Kelly Austin, Hoa and Phuong Nguyen, and Christine Peters.

Finally, I can't express enough gratitude for my husband and business partner, Gene Radeka, one of the best decisions I've ever made. In the past year, he has embraced the challenge of working out how to scale up from a one-person consulting firm with a limited number of clients so that we can help more companies get their best ideas to market faster. This book is the first fruit of that effort.

INDEX

ABOUT THE AUTHOR

Katherine Radeka is the founder and executive director of the Rapid Learning Cycles Institute, and supports a growing global community of Rapid Learning Cycles Certified® Professionals who are actively using the framework to get their best ideas to market faster.

She has worked with companies on every continent except Antarctica, and in industries such as aerospace, medical devices, pharmaceuticals, consumer electronics, and alternative energy.

In 2015, Katherine published the first edition of *The Shortest Distance Between You and Your New Product*. In 2012, she published the Shingo Research Award–winning book *The Mastery of Innovation*, based upon her research into Lean methods for product development.

Katherine has climbed seven of the tallest peaks in the Cascade Mountains and spent ten days alone on the Pacific Crest Trail until an encounter with a bear convinced her that she needed a change in strategic direction.